FRAMEWORK THINKING

Lessons in Community Planning and Design

WILLIAM J. JOHNSON
HAR YE KAN

Foreword by Charles A. Birnbaum

ORO EDITIONS

ORO Editions
Publishers of Architecture, Art, and Design
Gordon Goff: Publisher

www.oroeditions.com
info@oroeditions.com

Published by ORO Editions

Author: William J. Johnson and Har Ye Kan
Book Design: CircularStudio – Pablo Mandel, Gustavo Ibarra
Project Manager: Jake Anderson

Typeset in Scala Sans and Lyon Text

10 9 8 7 6 5 4 3 2 1 First Edition

ISBN: 978-1-961856-68-4

Prepress and Print work by ORO Editions Inc.
Printed in China

ORO Editions makes a continuous effort to minimize the overall carbon footprint of its publications. As part of this goal, ORO, in association with Global ReLeaf, arranges to plant trees to replace those used in the manufacturing of the paper produced for its books. Global ReLeaf is an international campaign run by American Forests, one of the world's oldest nonprofit conservation organizations. Global ReLeaf is American Forests' education and action program that helps individuals, organizations, agencies, and corporations improve the local and global environment by planting and caring for trees.

Finally, brothers and sisters, whatever is true, whatever is noble, whatever is right, whatever is pure, whatever is lovely, whatever is admirable—if anything is excellent or praiseworthy—think about such things.

—Philippians 4:8

To our families,
—Bill Johnson & Har Ye Kan

And Peter Walker, who helped me early in my life.
—Bill Johnson

A special thanks to Mark Tanis
for his friendship and creative energy
—Bill Johnson & Har Ye Kan

FOREWORD. Charles A. Birnbaum –9

PREFACE –13

ACKNOWLEDGMENTS –15

INTRODUCTION –17

A ROAD MAP –25

CHAPTER ONE **THE WORKPLACE CHALLENGE** –35

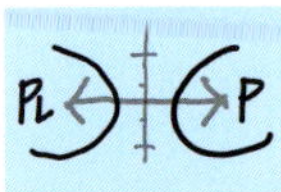

THE BASIC EQUATION –36

The basic global challenge of properly fitting human needs to natural conditions.

CHAPTER TWO **UNDERSTANDINGS** –47

THE PLAYING FIELD –48

The interesting range of options available for shaping unique career directions.

EARLY, EARLY, EARLY –54

The great advantage of the earliest possible involvement in building and preservation initiatives.

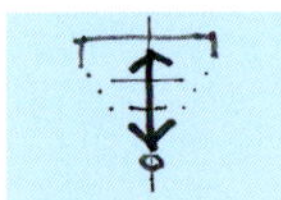

THE BIG CANVAS –60

Noting there are few limitations in project scale and magnitude.

CHAPTER THREE **PROCESS** –65

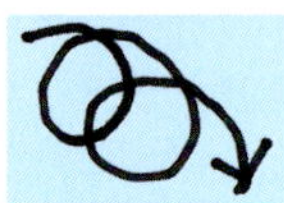

THE SEARCH –66

An iterative way of working, emphasizing probing, exploratory, and collaborative thinking.

VISIONS –76

An inspiring glimpse of a hoped-for outcome. It is the beginning of a search for physical development goals that match long-term aspirations and community values.

CHAPTER FOUR **DISCOVERY** –85

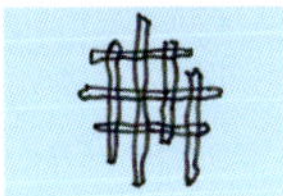

THE BONES –86

Emphasizing connecting networks of infrastructure and open space systems.

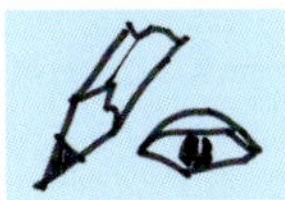

SPATIAL LANGUAGE –98

Lucid, quick sketches to sharpen early understandings and induce easy exchange of ideas.

CHAPTER FIVE **RESOLUTION** –111

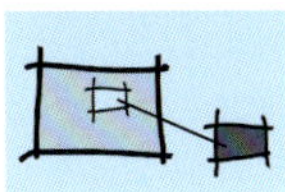

DESIGN AS FORM –112

The emergence of creative form driven by context understandings. The best final form is found, not prescribed.

CHAPTER SIX **INSIGHTS: FRAMEWORK UNDERSTANDINGS** –138

Three "difference makers" to strengthen the design thinking process and the key role of bridging between mindsets.

EPILOGUE **BRIDGE BUILDING & NEW LEARNINGS** –144

Consideration of emerging issues and learning priorities for stronger bridge building.

JOHNSON, JOHNSON & ROY, INC. (JJR): AN OVERVIEW –159

ENDNOTES –163

"A profession of edges [such as landscape architecture] is a tough one to work with. It's elusive and not always clear, but that's part of the territory."
—Bill Johnson on design, Pioneers Oral Histories Series with The Cultural Landscape Foundation, 2015

A Master's Recipe for Engaging with the Built Environment

Charles A. Birnbaum, FASLA, FAAR, president + CEO, The Cultural Landscape Foundation

Around 2015, The Cultural Landscape Foundation (TCLF) conducted a week-long oral history with Bill Johnson at his home and studio in Holland, Michigan, as well as at several mature projects in Ann Arbor and Grand Rapids. At that time, we on the production team had the good fortune to witness a planning and design leader at the top of his game and he privileged us with a master class. Bill revealed his process, which he called "Framework Thinking," and not only made it vastly accessible, but reflected on its refinement and fine-tuning throughout his career.

What was remarkable is that Bill, through his words and his process-heavy graphics and drawings, made it easy for us to understand and engage with his unique approach to people and places—one that could be characterized as open and transparent. As our week together came to close, Bill reflected on more than a half century of practice, proclaiming with great excitement, "Wouldn't it be great if there was [a] more integrative thought when problem solving by our architecture friends and our engineering friends and those who do urban planning and design? Wouldn't it be great? I think it's legitimate to say it isn't happening now—but wouldn't it be great?"

This quest for collaboration, and the critical role that landscape architects are positioned to play as "difference-makers," as Bill put it, has been at the forefront of his work ever since he graduated from the landscape architecture program at Michigan State University, Lansing in 1954, and throughout his career.

Context: Bill Briefly

To understand Bill's unique approach, it is important to understand his professional evolution. Following his military service in 1956, Bill completed a master's in landscape architecture at the Harvard University Graduate School of Design (GSD) during which time he worked for Hideo Sasaki while also serving as an instructor at the GSD. He returned to the Midwest and co-founded Johnson, Johnson & Roy, Inc. (JJR) in 1961, with his brother Carl and friend Clarence Roy. The firm's master plan for the University of Michigan in Ann Arbor significantly raised JJR's visibility and positioning for work, and broadcast Bill's ambition and strategic philosophy that prioritized fitness, harmony, and community engagement (built on a foundation of careful listening) as critical to context sensitive planning and design.

This core planning/design philosophy underpinned Bill's professional practice at JJR (1961–75), Willam J. Johnson Associates (1980–92), and at Peter Walker William Johnson and Partners (1992–97), in addition to his myriad academic engagements, first as a professor of landscape architecture (1958) and later as dean of the School of Natural Resources at the University of Michigan (1975–83). Perhaps Bill's greatest acknowledgment for his work came in 1986 when he received the American Society of Landscape Architects' Medal, the highest honor bestowed by the society.

Context: The Profession Briefly

To understand the state of the profession during this time and to contextualize both the opportunity and appetite for Bill's methodologies, one must recognize that there was a seismic shift taking place in landscape architecture. This period was marked by the passing of hugely influential figures: Ellen Shipman (1950), Jens Jensen (1951), Frederick Law Olmsted, Jr. (1957) and Beatrix Farrand (1959).

Coming out of the military, Bill was aware of the country's severe housing shortage, and, as a graduate of the GSD, he understood the potential role that modernism could play. At this time, Hideo Sasaki, who as a student had been influenced by Walter Gropius, the GSD's dean (1937–52), became chair of the landscape architecture program. The program's graduates would become leaders of modernist design: Thomas Church, Garrett Eckbo, Lawrence Halprin, Dan Kiley, James Rose, John Simonds, Bob Zion, and Johnson's classmate, Peter Walker. These practitioners fundamentally redefined the profession by moving away from gardens and estates to new landscape typologies that included plazas and roof decks; pedestrian malls; corporate, cultural, and academic campuses; new types of parks (vest pocket, neighborhood, and urban waterfront); and residential subdivisions, all designed to cater to postwar urbanities and suburbanites.

As Peter Walker and Melanie Simo noted in *Invisible Gardens: The Search for Modernism in the American Landscape* (1994): "Sasaki's effect on students was more cerebral, yet no less personal and inspiring. In 1950, he looked beyond the teaching methods at hand ... At schools' intent on guiding the cutting edge of the profession, the professor of landscape architecture would assume the roles of manager, coordinator, and critic." These are the very roles that Sasaki, Walker, and Johnson adopt in their academic and private sector endeavors.[1]

Furthermore, with these stylistic and leadership innovations taking hold, imagine the opportunity that Bill saw (and seized upon) in developing and refining his approach to Framework Thinking. To understand its place in the planning and design process, here is how Bill summarized the situation in TCLF's 2015 oral history:

> *As I consider this kind of territory, my own bias brings me strongly over to the social sciences and I include in that the architectural world, the engineering world. That's where I hover. My work is not primarily art, as such, it's design. It's the solving of a challenge and [that] process takes me over to the social sciences more. I'm not a natural scientist or even close to being a pseudo-scientist. I lean on those guys big time to help what I do be solid and dependable, as I lean on the art world to help me in whatever I'm doing to not only create something that's artful, but to help others help me be artful ... It says in a way that design is a big deal as a way of thinking with capital letters.* ***It's not only form producing but process sensitive*** *[emphasis added].*[2]

Throughout his career, and captured in *Framework Thinking*, Bill encourages us to invite/welcome debate, and, most critically, to think—and act—holistically. He challenges us by asking are we "able, as a professional, to help [in the public] arena to see possible ideas? Possible outcomes that aren't immediately available to people who are just arguing, but that say wow, not only can I make my argument, but this could be an outcome. And the more quickly that's done on the spot, which takes skill, the better the debate and the more, the further you can reach toward an idea that is prevalent."[3]

Context: Looking Outside of the Disciplines

Framework Thinking is accessible and easy to understand through its straightforward text and evocative graphics. The same could be said about a book published in 1961, the same year JJR was founded: *Mastering the Art of French Cooking*. In the latter, authors Simone Beck, Louisette Bertholle, and Julia Child tackled the topic by breaking down the subject's inherent challenges into its fundamentals, while also inviting its readers to master their techniques and philosophical principles. *Framework Thinking* does the same in its discussion of the community design and planning process.

Moreover, Child and Johnson are both affable, accessible, and masters of their respective arts eager to share what they know and empower their readers with that knowledge.

Bill's curiosity, and his love of people is open-ended and in producing this exceptional work—a gift, really—he and collaborator Har Ye Kan honor their commitment to learning as a shared value. Whether you're a layperson or seasoned professional community builder, *Framework Thinking* will prove both eye-opening and revelatory.

So, as Julia would say, *bon appétit.*

PREFACE

HAVING BEEN involved in every corner of the urban planning and design field for well over 60 years, I keep bumping into what we professionals call "difference makers"... some unique problem-solving practices that promise extraordinary outcomes. It is a common experience among fellow teachers and practitioners, and we all are on the alert to find them.

Early in my career, I came across what turned out for me to be the most significant of these difference-makers. It was about the importance of holistic thinking ... putting all elements into the context of the circumstances at hand. We later called this mindset Framework Thinking. It was a distinguishing feature ever since in projects of every type and scale.

A key element was the skill of building a "Vision"—how the Vision is found, articulated, and sustained. What has intrigued me is learning the importance of a Vision, yet knowing as well how elusive a Vision is to define and use.

There is a point in the problem-solving process where the broad Vision-building view narrows to the shaping of development form. At this point the power of the Vision as a guiding force is either confirmed or set aside, its absence unnoticed, and an opportunity for a more fitting outcome lost. Such a risk is not necessary.

The thrust of this book is to share with my community-building colleagues—civic leaders, private and nonprofit stewards, planning and design practitioners—about how one can increase the clarity, power, and enduring presence of an inspired Vision through a Framework Thinking process.

Working in concert with Har Ye Kan, AICP, I intend to illustrate what a Framework direction looks like, when it shows, and how to use it. Har Ye represents the recent generation while I represent the post-war generation, setting up a fitting combination to consider the impacts of current and potential future cultural change.

William J. Johnson, FASLA

ACKNOWLEDGMENTS

WE DEDICATE this book to our ***families and Peter Walker***. Without our families, we could not have done this and everything else in our professional lives. Pete was formative as a friend and classmate for Bill. He helped Bill sharpen his thinking and approach to planning and design. And Bill always said that if he ever were to write a book, he would dedicate it to Pete.

At Harvard, one of Bill's teachers was ***Hideo Sasaki*** and he joined with ***Peter Walker*** in representing a view of design that was all encompassing and full of value. Pete and Hideo each in their own way added words referring to the emergence of a planning and design direction. For Pete, it was "an idea". For Hideo, it was "structure". Bill will always remember that, and it is part of the vocabulary we now use every day.

Before ***Carl Johnson*** and ***Clarence Roy*** passed, all the Framework Thinking elements Johnson, Johnson, and Roy (JJR) had, and all the victories foretold were predictable because of partners like them. They were quick, they were insightful, and they became unforgettable.

A unique person that fortunately provided invaluable support at times when a creative view of publications reveals its content is graphic artist ***Mark Tanis***. We are thankful for our weekly coffee breaks and friendships with him.

In preparing such a book the people who walk into the arena to help clarify and enlarge the story in a proper way continue to emerge.

Greg Holcombe's involvement was not only with the application of the Framework Thinking principles, but also giving thoughtful, continuous feedback during the process of writing this book.

Ed Mickelson and ***Sandy Fischer*** are veterans of the Design Process. They quickly understood the intent of Framework Thinking, adding much of the dialogue. Their help in keeping the proper flow of the message was immeasurable. We are so very grateful.

Charles Birnbaum has the unique ability of seeing design implications and broad strategic plans. He is an invaluable asset to the design firms around the country. We have been gifted by his enthusiastic support for the principles of Framework Thinking.

Jim Richards is a faithful supporter of the professions' planning and design principles. He has given us excellence, encouragement, and insights.

Additionally, we are blessed with several valuable friends and colleagues who were generous with their time, constructive comments, and encouragement: ***Bob Chipman, Bob Grese, Nate Young, David Knibbe, Ed DeNuve & Randy Bouto***.

We want to express our appreciation to ***Gordon Goff, Jake Anderson, and the ORO Editions team*** for their enthusiastic interest, patient advice, and belief in the purpose and vision for the book. ***Pablo Mandel***'s graphic design talents crystalized everything in more ways than what we could have imagined.

This journey was also made possible with the wise advice and professional expertise of others. ***Ann Smith***, our copyeditor and friend, joined us readily with her careful review and keen eye to make this an accessible read. ***Peter G. Rowe***, Har Ye's long-time mentor and Raymond Garbe Distinguished Service Professor at the Harvard GSD, provided his experienced insights on the publishing world.

In casting visions and making projects a reality, blending the transformational with the transactional in a manner that constantly raises the bar, we have depended on the good, enriching thoughts of many ***collaborators and community leaders***. We would like to acknowledge all of them as well as those who we worked with on the projects featured here.

Unless otherwise noted, all drawings, sketches, and diagrams are the work of William J. Johnson, FASLA. The source for other illustrations which were used with the generosity of others is noted with the respective item. We would like to thank ***The Cultural Landscape Foundation, PWWI (Peter Walker William Johnson & Associates)/PWP Landscape Architecture, NBBJ, GMB, Prairie Crossing, Johnson Hill Land Ethics Studio, and the Crystal Mountain Resort***, for providing the permissions to use various photographs and illustrations.

Every effort has been made to contact and credit the copyright holders of all other materials. In a few cases, we have not received any responses. We apologize for any potential infringements which may have inadvertently occurred. Please contact us if there are any questions on attribution.

Finally, this book could not have been written without the moral support of ***Denny and Scoob Ellens***. Their invitation to Bill to be part of the community here in Holland, Michigan, was the start of everything. Their quiet presence and thoughtful encouragement have meant the world to him. Bill is so grateful they have been part of his life for so many years! They hover above it all.

INTRODUCTION

Shaping places in which people live and gather is an art as old as human existence. How it is done, and in what form, follows the ebb and flow of history, leaving countless examples today of cities, towns, and villages to ponder. All are a product of their time.

In recent years, shaping or reshaping community is often referred to as some form of urban planning or community building. For those involved, it is intriguing to see various interest groups come together, exchange ideas, and work through to final conclusions. It is a process continually being refined to be as effective as possible.

Framework Thinking is about lessons learned in the community building process and how that process might be improved. These lessons became the "difference makers" in Bill's career and the longstanding success of Johnson, Johnson & Roy, Inc. (JJR)—an innovative, interdisciplinary planning and design firm Bill established with Carl Johnson and Clarence Roy in 1961. Now part of SmithGroup, JJR first conceptualized the "Framework" approach in the 1960s that later became widely adopted in the planning and design professions.

The *basic ingredients for design excellence* were discovered early, prior to the JJR partnership. Each element is represented by a unique icon. Collectively, they form the arc of this book.

The *focus of these difference makers* is on the *first half* of a planning/design *process* leading to the *"Framework Directions."* It is where the nine icons cultivate a *"way of working"* aimed at identifying various interests

FIG. 1: Basic ingredients for design excellence — Nine icons and principles of Framework Thinking.

and guiding them to formulate long-held hopes and aspirations—a "Vision." The intent is to frame the Vision as a set of directional guidelines by about the midpoint of the overall process.

Such a process may seem rather simple at first but soon proves to be a complex, multi-layered challenge with many moving parts.

The process this book describes is fundamentally a sequence of findings, moving from "understanding the need" to an action-oriented decision, often in the form of "build" outcomes. Along the way, as findings

FIG. 2: Typical planning & design process with iterative feedback loops.

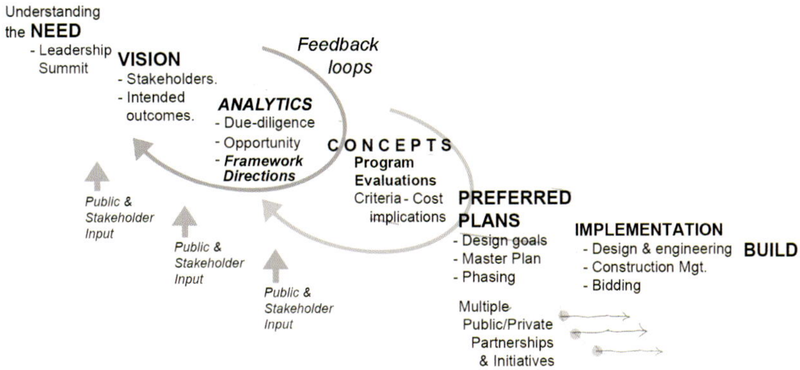

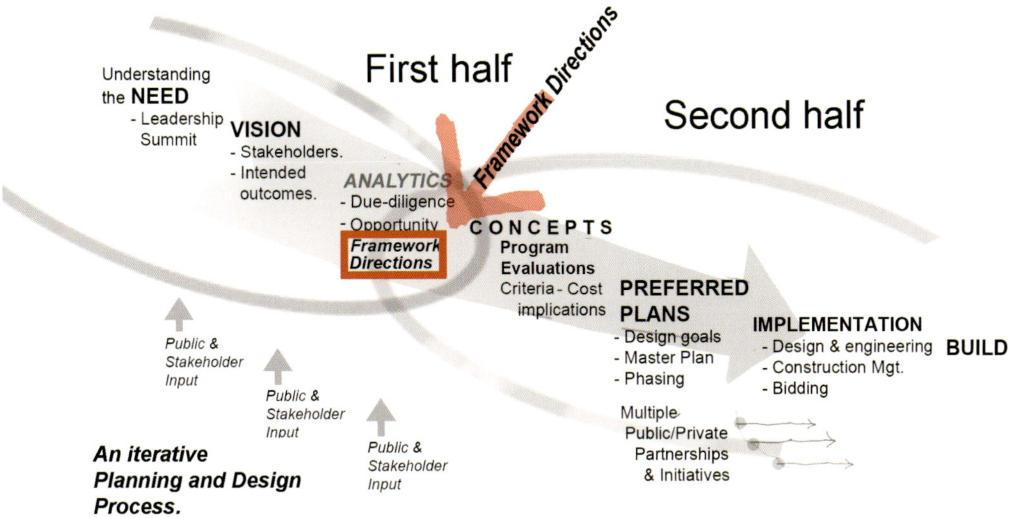

FIG. 3: Visionary focus in the first half of the process culminating in the Framework Directions at a critical point of Bridging with the Implementation focus in the second half.

begin to emerge, iterative feedback loops support double-checking earlier assumptions.

Just as vital is the *second half* of the process—the *"Implementation" focus*—which extends beyond the emphasis of the nine icons. A *key message of this book is the call to bridge two different mindsets —the "transformational" (visionary) and "transactional" (pragmatic)*. That involves an intentional effort to meld the best of both approaches. These two types of leadership are noted by American presidential historian

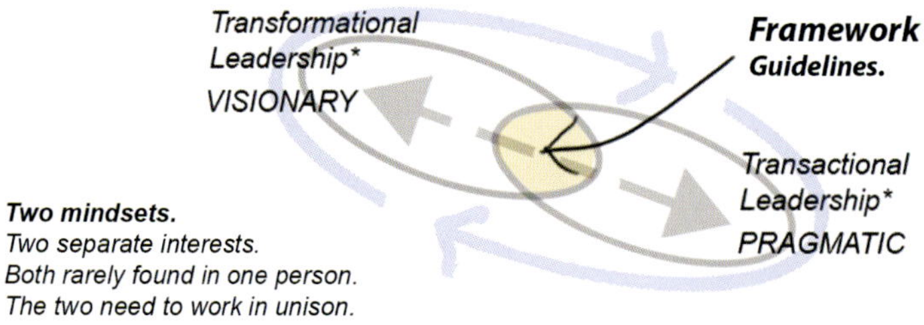

FIG. 4: The transformational and transactional mindsets in leadership per Doris Kearns Goodwins.

Doris Kearns Goodwin about Abraham Lincoln's extraordinary gifts in enlarging the lives of the people for a greater purpose while holding a divided country together.[4]

While it is rare to find both the visionary and pragmatic mindsets in a single person, Goodwin's call—and our belief—is that bridging is essentially an exercise in leadership, which can be cultivated both in the design process and with the community/client. To this end, *Framework Thinking* concludes with a summary of *emergent Framework understandings* and some thoughts on *bridging and process leadership*, while considering ongoing major shifts in environmental and cultural values.

Why It Matters and Where It Began

Over the last 60 years, *Framework Thinking* has been proven to bring meaning to community visioning, strength to the design of places, and efficiency to the creative process.

The roots of this Framework approach can be traced to several turning points in Bill's career. The first was his encounter with Hideo Sasaki, who invited him to join the landscape architecture program at the Harvard Graduate School of Design (GSD). A pioneer in integrated design and collaborative interdisciplinary approaches, Sasaki's principles were formative. In studio reviews and projects, he was able to listen to all points of view and quickly sum things up. To Sasaki, any robust design outcomes hinged on one question: *"What is the structure of the place?"*

The second turning point occurred at Harvard, where Peter Walker, Bill's GSD classmate, quickly became a kindred spirit about the analytic process. He would come over, look at Bill's work, and say, "Well, this looks OK, but *what's your idea?*" For Bill (and later, JJR), the *"Bones"* of a place became the basic structure in figuring out optimal possibilities, whether a project is natural systems oriented or focused on the cultural values or the technology of infrastructure influencing the way a city works. What are the *Bones*? What are the *fundamentals*? It is a point of view that says if we can determine the fundamental frame in physical terms, you are well equipped to add flesh in good places and help correct mistakes fast. It takes discipline to avoid glossing over this too quickly, which can result in missing opportunities to discover the potential of a place.

A third turning point can be traced to the University of Michigan's Central Campus planning efforts in 1963. Asked to take on a study of a long-term campus development plan for the institution in the 1960s, Bill, Carl, and Clarence took an inside-out approach. Departing from the Beaux Arts plans prevalent at that time, with grand vistas and formal building arrangements, they focused instead on the spaces and connections between buildings rather than the shape of the buildings. Their efforts give rise to the comprehensive Framework plan for the University of Michigan. Both the plan and the analytics consequently epitomized the Framework Thinking approach.

The Framework or Bones were developed by closely observing the historic, natural, cultural, and utility patterns of the place. The Framework based on "academic avenues" fit well with the institution's need to flexibly adapt and evolve to support a variety of building forms, functions, and densities. This fresh way of thinking was communicated broadly throughout the country and became commonly referred to as the "Framework plan."

Since then, in place of piecemeal, cookie-cutter development that reflects a comfort with mediocrity, JJR's *Framework Thinking* approach has yielded processes and projects that raised the bar for the communities they served. They are distinguished by:

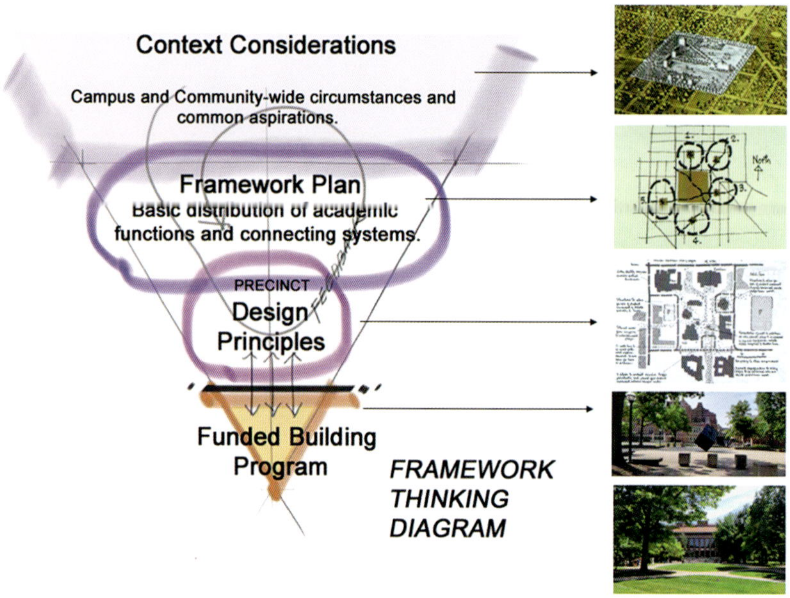

FIG. 5: The University of Michigan Central Campus Plan (c.1963) showing how contextual understandings shape the Vision and Framework, leading to smaller-scale design and implementation outcomes.

- Overall clarity in the integration and connectivity within the proposed development, as well as with its broader context, through greenways, walkways, bikeways, and roadways.
- Careful, respectful balance between people and nature.
- A thoughtful fit with the context and culture.
- The involvement, awareness, and embrace of development leaders and associated community members to advance the Vision long after it was first cast.
- Innate momentum and shared understanding with the client and community to push the limits, within constraints, to achieve exceptional, impactful outcomes.

In recent years, Bill's continued conversations with fellow professionals contemplated current relevance and future implications of *Framework*

Thinking. As the explorations evolved, it became clear there is still an unmet need for holistic approaches to building more livable communities.

Amidst accelerated climate change, environmental concerns have also sharpened, paving the way for sustainability and resiliency considerations.[5] The desire for connectivity—both physical and social—has reframed design approaches to infrastructure.[6] Most urban communities are more diverse than ever before and a broad concern for social and ecological justice has prompted stronger calls for inclusiveness.[7] And the digital revolution has pressed new demands for transparency, new ways of listening and engagement—and, more recently with artificial intelligence (AI), new forms of creative production.

With COVID-19, our experience and perceptions of the built environment have also been fundamentally transformed. Issues of proximity, working remotely and connecting digitally, and the value of outdoor spaces and natural environments raised new questions about uses, programming, planning, design, and operations. Accompanying a renewed attention to health and wellbeing[8] is the growing desire for safe, active public spaces.[9] Above all is a common, unwavering aspiration to elevate quality of life, to belong, and to engender a shared sense of place—a sense of community—wherever that may be.

It is increasingly clear that to successfully achieve these ends calls for more integrative and innovative ways of thinking beyond the norm. Working creatively in concert across public and private interests is a major challenge in a free-market economy. The dominance of single-purpose initiatives such as housing, transportation, or managing the rise in sea level complicates working in unison. So does the tendency to rush to detail in projects, which often bypasses overview thinking that is critical in early, contextual analysis. A more deliberate approach to visionary thinking is a much-needed step in the right direction.

What follows is a series of reflections on *Framework Thinking*, connecting the past, present, and future. Woven throughout are memories, anecdotes, and project examples from our professional experiences—stories which we hope offer meaning and revelations beyond the key ideas. The stories are told in two voices. In tracing the arc from past to present, Bill's reflections and recollections assume a personal voice.

In projecting from the present to the future and to capture the spirit of our conversations, we shift to a collective voice. Because of Bill's roots in landscape architecture, references are sometimes made to the discipline. Yet it becomes clear that the precepts, process, and projects here quickly transcend disciplinary boundaries. They blur the edges between planning and design, the large and the small scales, and buildings and elements of the land.

In blending these insights, our hope is to offer an accessible process that maintains a "big picture" point of view for the thoughtful shaping of communities. Consciously or unconsciously, the Framework Thinking elements represented by the nine icons are already part of every problem-solving process. In so doing, perhaps *Framework Thinking* can add a small, intriguing crease in the greater body of work on placemaking.[10] The lessons learned, we believe, can offer us a way forward to the stewardship of the good we have in common by making the little choices to dig deeper and think bigger.

A ROAD MAP

Key Terms

The term "Framework" encourages a *broad view of the conditions and circumstances surrounding a planning/design problem*. It is an attitude about and awareness of the wholeness of a community, the kind that calls for a view that builds creative dialogue and energizes the shaping of an effective, long-term Vision as different interest groups gather to explore the solutions to a perceived *need*.

This deliberate problem-solving approach can apply to any scale of a building need but the reference here is more expansive. We are speaking of a significant area in a community, such as neighborhood preservation, downtown renewal, campus planning, resort planning, transportation corridor improvements, or waterfront development. In terms of time horizons, it is a *blending of long- and short-term insights and realities*.

The *Framework Thinking* process has two things at its center: *collaboration and authentic engagement*. It is all about teamwork, attentive listening, and easy involvement. Stakeholders' resulting dialogue about ideas is central to creating an enduring Vision. Building together on conversations and their takeaways, stakeholders can synthesize emergent thoughts into compelling ideas and potential future directions.

These early elements are the building blocks of a *Vision—an inspiring glimpse of a hoped-for outcome*. It serves as *a kind of North Star*, providing a quietly persistent, clear, and ready reference point to where a community is headed and why. In written terms, it is a succinct statement that describes a prospect rising above the daily grind while suggesting a future that seems to fit the tangible realities.

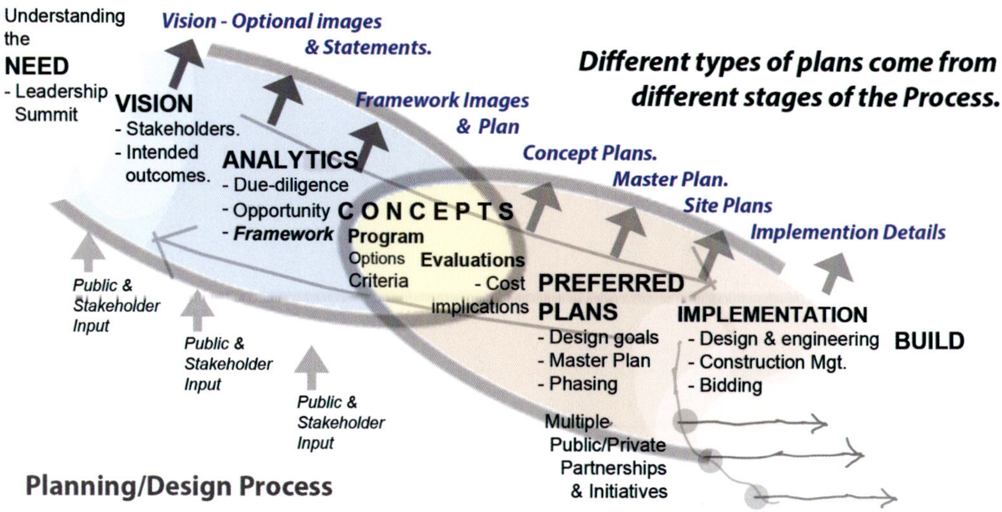

In the planning and design process, a Vision diagram drawn to scale and combined with a short narrative constitute a Framework plan. Together with a set of guiding principles, they complete the Framework Directions. This foundational document subsequently informs the implementation process with its familiar master plan. The difference is that the Framework Directions focus on long-term policy while the master plan is directed at short-term building design and construction.

FIG. 6: Typical planning and design process showing the different types of plans at various stages.

For example, the following is the 1989 Downtown Vision Statement accompanied by a Framework diagram for Downtown Holland, Michigan. To this day, some thirty years later, it continues to be the basic guide to future central city form.

THE DOWNTOWN HOLLAND VISION STATEMENT

A New Kind of Destination Downtown.
A PLACE of distinction, where quality shops and residential life co-mingle, where campus functions blend with the urban center, where tiny green places provide respite, where waterfronts are lined with greenways and walkability is a priority. This is the spirit of the kind of Downtown we seek.

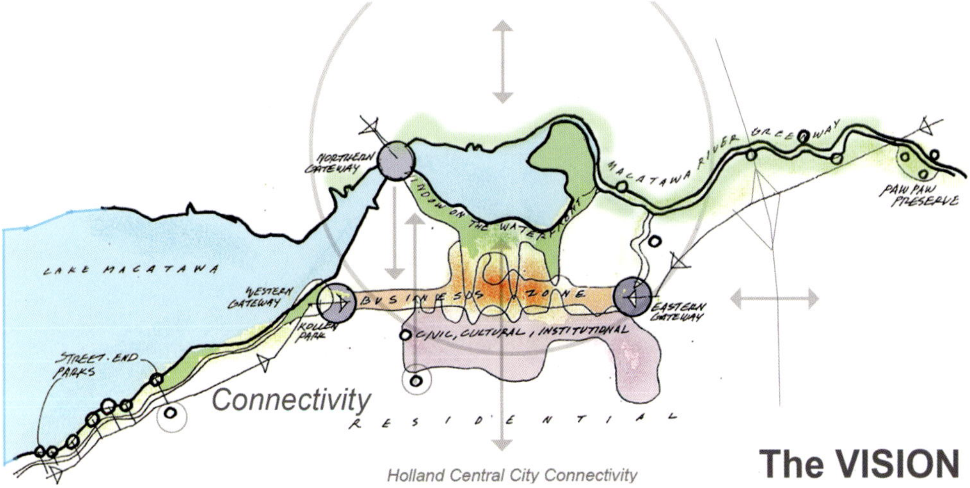

FIG. 7: The Downtown Holland Vision diagram (c1990).

The statement is visually conveyed in this diagram from 1990 outlining the fundamental aspirations of the downtown plan for Holland, Michigan. At its heart is the theme of "connectivity." Much of this long-term hope has been achieved and it remains a guide.

Once a Vision statement is drafted and has been refined with affirmation from most stakeholders, the *key is to keep it on the table*. With the complexities and demands of the later building stages, it is only natural that any Vision can fade from view. Accordingly, it is important to find disciplined ways to keep the Vision active and in the forefront of planning and discussions. The best chance of advancing, sharpening, and sustaining the Vision lies in community leaders—public and private—who join in carrying it forward. This can be cultivated early and maintained throughout the process, fostering a familiarity with and belief in its long-term development guidance. The intention is that it can be referenced with ease and confidence. The Vision could be a one-page summary, an overview board, or some handy postcards.

Finally, *Framework Thinking* is *both intangible and tangible*. Besides the *tangible Framework Directions* that are drawn and articulated, it is also an *intangible mindset* such that an awareness of the larger context is ever present even when one is working down in the weeds. Some find this

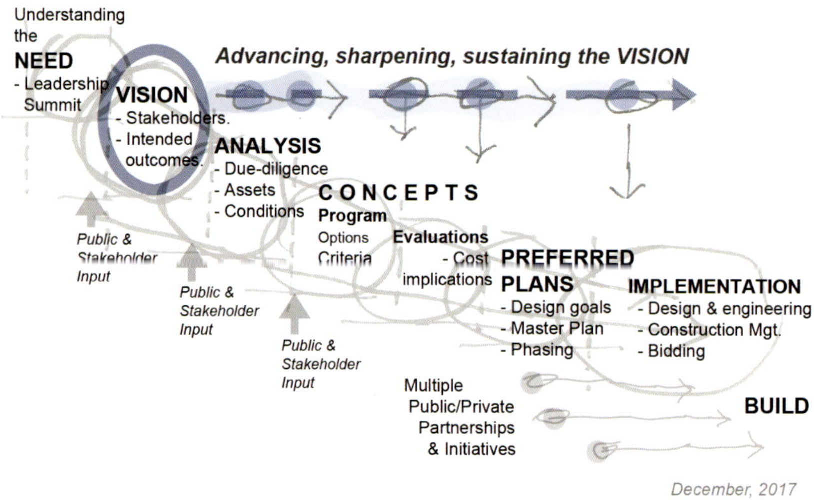

FIG. 8: The key is to sustain, sharpen, and advance the Vision over time.

big picture awareness built into their makeup, but others find such larger-scale generalities too elusive. This reflects an inherent fragility in the planning/design process, which is susceptible to the pulls of two quite different mindsets: the visionary (early in the process) and the pragmatic (later in the process). *Framework Thinking* is thus a bridge intended to achieve unison between the two.

A Road Map

The book is organized by the design precepts fundamental to a broad-based approach to the design of places for people. Chapters One to Five outline the elements of *Framework Thinking: Challenges, Understandings, Process, Discovery, and Resolution.* These basic ingredients for design excellence are identified with one or two simple icons. The first five chapters describe the icons in detail. Each icon represents a special skill or insight to strengthen holistic thinking by a broad base of design-related understandings.

THE WORKPLACE CHALLENGE

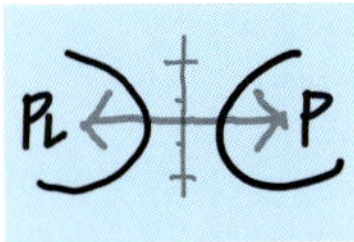

The Basic Equation

Chapter One: Challenges explains "The Basic Equation"—the tension between the limited carrying capacity of the Earth and the relentless advance of growth and urbanization. It suggests potential areas where a planning and design practitioner could strive to find a sustainable fit to resolve the conflicts between the two fundamental challenges. Looking into the future, this chapter situates the "People–Place" challenge within the "People–Place–Prosperity" paradigm of sustainability.

UNDERSTANDINGS

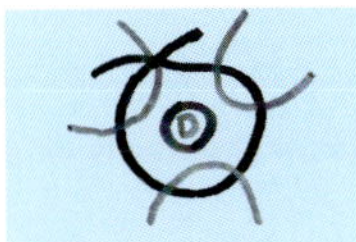

The Playing Field

Early, Early, Early

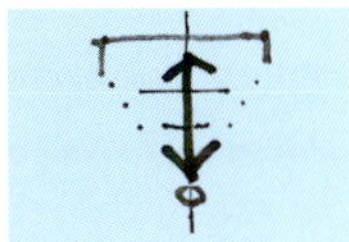

The Big Canvas

Chapter Two: Understandings delves into the professional awareness that could be cultivated before the problem-solving process begins. Three elements are central here: "The Playing Field," "Leverage" or "Early, Early, Early," and "The Big Canvas." The Playing Field suggests a mindfulness of a multidisciplinary team approach and of one's professional identity, fit, and role within the design disciplines and associated fields. It is about understanding the breadth of the planning and design disciplines and avoiding later confusion as to who you think you are and where you serve. It is quickly clear that little can be accomplished without other professions and disciplines being involved from the start, pointing to the idea of *teamwork* being the working norm.

Leverage, or Early, Early, Early, is a reminder to become involved early in the game (through demonstrated issue awareness, proposal-making, or contract arrangements), thereby increasing leverage and influence. This icon recognizes the dilemma landscape architects often face when drawn in only at the end of the design process. To influence the important Vision-building stages, they must learn to be there early and be ready to lead as needed. This is not about being boastful, but about applying early the learned inclinations to think at the site and regional scales, all from a creative design point of view.

Drawing on the characteristics of natural systems, the Big Canvas alludes to the development of a broad contextual sensitivity and a proficiency to *shift easily between extensive scale variations*. One day it can be a public square design, the next day it can be a natural systems preservation strategy. Given that landscape architects' education is based in natural systems, their role, in part, is to represent a design-oriented bridging discipline between the natural sciences and the building professions of architecture and engineering. Such a role, blending larger-scale thinking and smaller design details, is often missing in development and design initiatives.

With more complex issues to be resolved, the early assemblage of a multidisciplinary team with different perspectives can support a blend of big-picture aspirations and detailed pragmatics, and a balance between long-term impacts and short-term wins. In the same vein, because there will be many involved in the implementation process, enabling them to contribute to and embrace the Vision early gives it a greater chance of sustaining and succeeding.

PROCESS

The Search

Visions

Building on the two earlier tenets, Chapters Three to Five focus on the various ways design is activated. Chapter Three: Process unpacks the principles that defined JJR's practice. Its two icons are important reminders when entering the problem-solving process. "The Search" describes an iterative, analytical, and creative problem-solving process that has been practiced, taught, and proven effective over the past 60 years. This

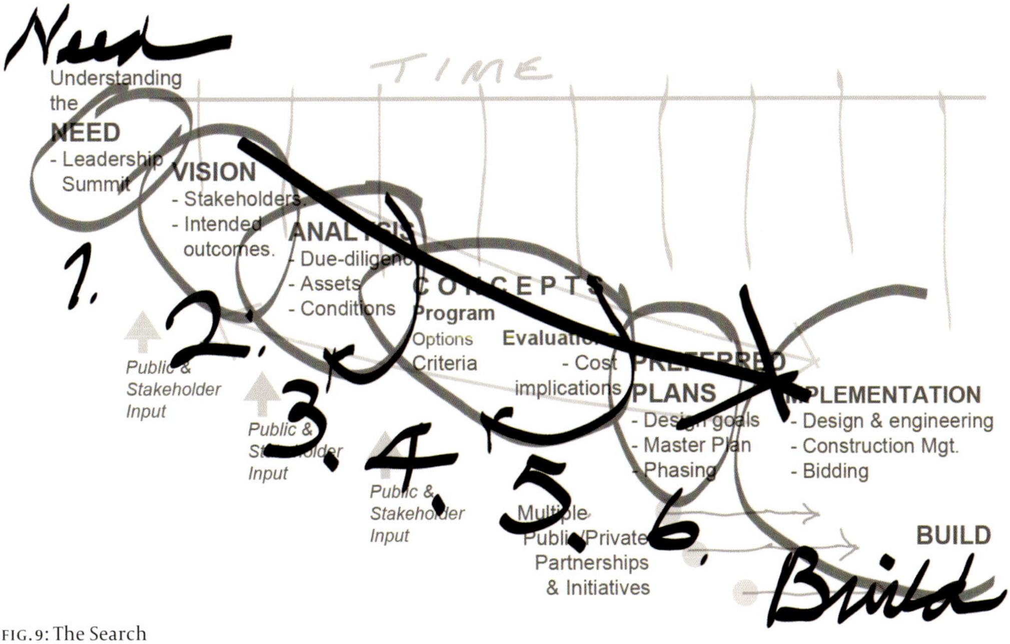

FIG. 9: The Search through an iterative, analytical and creative problem-solving process.

deliberate series of steps assure looseness, structure, and order amid creative discourse and openness to surprises.

"Visions" in this chapter are first about a *Vision-building process*—discovering among the stakeholders and working team a range of hopes and aspirations about the future. Establishing a set of evaluation criteria along the way is a priority. While it is a common feature of planning and design, Visioning is not always easily accomplished or sustained. Secondly, Visions are also about *tangible outcomes*—narrative statements and spatial diagrams that clearly describe the emergent Vision of choice and align it with Framework summaries. The first implications of a *design direction* are revealed, and care is taken to focus on the "Frame" of a potential plan, not the specific form.

DISCOVERY

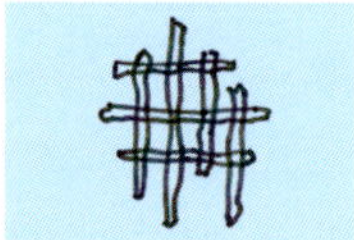

The Bones

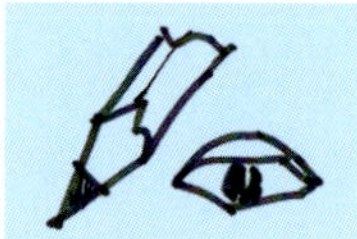

Spatial Language

Chapter Four: Discovery explores "The Bones" and "Spatial Language," the two cornerstones of Framework Thinking. The term "Bones" implies "Frame"—the basic, physical direction of a Vision derived from a holistic viewpoint. The Bones describe the specific nature of framework plans, the dynamics of how it is incrementally built, and why a distinctive spatial language is such a help.

To discover this preferred long-term direction, there is a natural, intuitive use of hand-drawn graphics. The simple medium of quick pencil sketches for idea exploration, on-the-spot dialogue facilitation, and visual communication is powerful. Through sketching, the simultaneous working of hand–heart–mind supports an integral thinking represented by the Framework. With the digital landscape, many tools of choice have evolved, yet the lessons learnt by drawing have not. The Frame is a means to realize the pieces of the key idea within the bigger picture. Similarly, Spatial Language is a means to discover potential solutions. Together, they encourage collaborative probing with key stakeholders. An easy yet often overlooked part in the design process, finding the Bones and expressing them with a spatial language are the crux of this book.

RESOLUTION

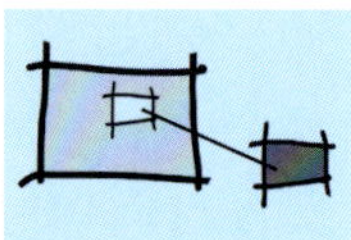

Form Discovery

Chapter Five: Resolution rounds out the nine design principles with Form Discovery. This is likely the most familiar and focused outcome for planning and design professionals. What sets this principle apart is its intentionality in shaping places of distinction consistent with the vision—creating a detailed, form-based summary expressing the key insights gained in the earlier process work. It also emphasizes the importance of a context mindset and identifies the design characteristics commonly considered in distinctive urban design form.

Chapter Six: Insights rounds out the reflections and highlights three difference makers to strengthen the design thinking process and the key role of bridging between mindsets. In the Epilogue, we conclude with an invitation to look back on why we embarked on a conversation about *Framework Thinking* and why it matters for our future. It begins with contemplation about common concerns and cultures shaping development, design, and community building, and then considers the beginnings of hoped-for directions and attitudes among those broadly involved in the "place shaping" and "place keeping" world. To create more livable, sustainable futures, the design and planning professions—as well as community decision-makers—can foster the spirit of this Framework Thinking mindset by being a bridge.

CHAPTER ONE

THE WORKPLACE CHALLENGE

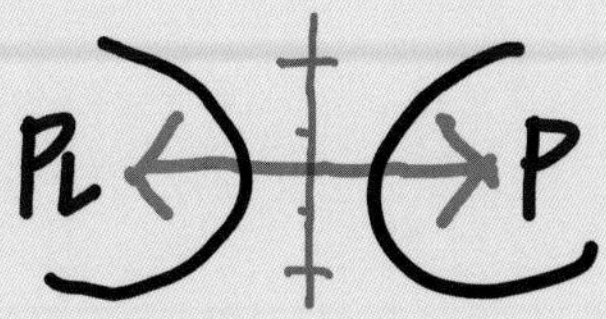

THE BASIC EQUATION

Earth/People in Tension—Seeking a Sustainable Fit

This icon describes the "Basic Equation" we all must face. The little diagram illustrates the intense collision between planet Earth's limited carrying capacity and the relentless advance of urbanization. The center is the working place where professionals gather to resolve inevitable conflicts. It behooves every practitioner to find their purpose in this equation—somewhere between advocate on either end or problem-solver in the middle. Environmental protection and restoration are commonly held values on both sides.

THE BASIC EQUATION

In the 1950s, graduate programs in architecture and land planning featured outstanding faculty. But just as important, perhaps more so, were the fellow students who gathered. They were from all over the country, if not the world. They had already excelled.

The Harvard Graduate School of Design (GSD) spawned student interactions outside the classroom. It was invigorating to gather frequently with a few others in spontaneous coffee breaks or over a late-night beer. Discussions and debates were often far-ranging. A new and growing concern at the time was rapid population growth and the limits of the Earth to safely accommodate such growth. I recall how energized we were to realize we were preparing to play a role in such an important global issue.

During those discussions, dozens of diagrams sketched out on paper napkins expressed a point of view or an idea. The hand-drawn one in Fig. 10 was sketched to illustrate the tension between development and preservation. Many other versions followed with increasing clarity, eventually culminating in the carefully crafted final refinement shown in Fig. 11. There are several parts to the diagram. Viewing them together, one can get an overall sense of the conflict, prospects of potential resolution, and the special role design professionals can play.

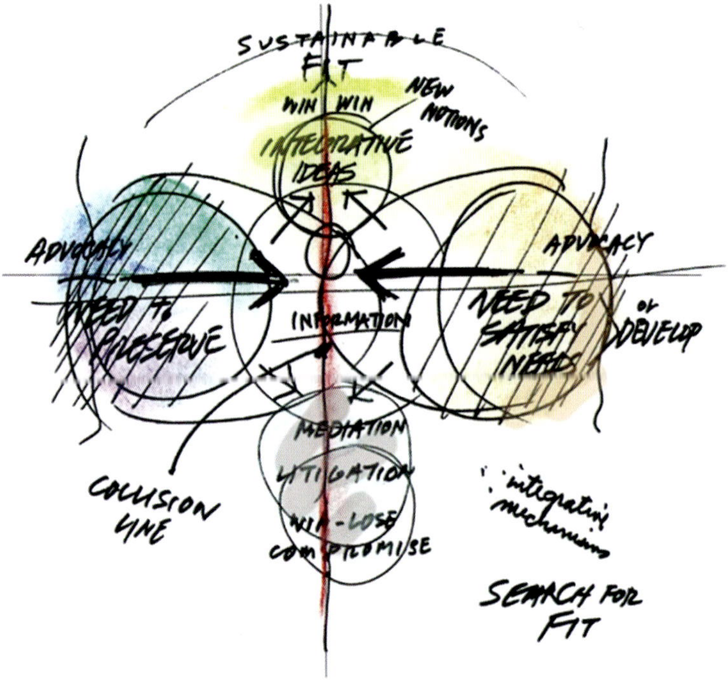

FIG. 10: An early napkin sketch of the Basic Equation showing the tension between development and preservation, and the search for a sustainable fit between the two.

This kind of clarity was crucial to me in the early 1960s while working with graduate students in land and community planning. Though a planner may be working at a tiny scale (such as a residential garden, campus walkways, or a neighborhood park), it is but a small part of a larger picture. One day they will inevitably work on issues with much higher stakes than first meet the eye. Then, the inclination and ability to put the larger picture into context will be worth its weight in gold.

The Basic Message the Diagram Represents

First, the diagram attempts to urge planning and design professionals to be aware of the significant impact urbanization has on the capacity of the Earth to sustain such an endeavor without undue damage.

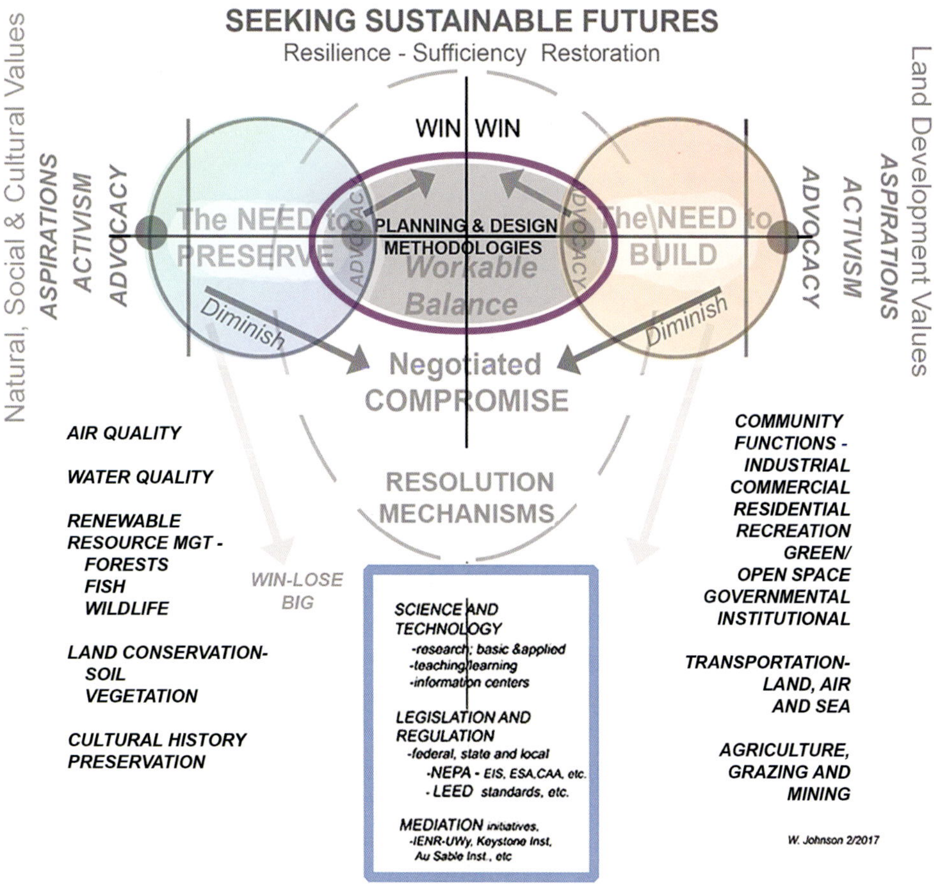

FIG. 11: A further refinement of the napkin sketch, showing the special role planning and design professionals can play in the middle in seeking win-win outcomes between preservation and development.

Second, it illustrates where on the spectrum of possible input the most productive role might occur.

Third, it emphasizes that a deliberate, interdisciplinary, and science-based process is essential in achieving positive outcomes. It includes the prospect for new ideas to be found, increasing chances for rare *win-win* outcomes.

Accordingly, the diagram shows two interest centers (development initiatives and environmental protection) set far apart on a horizontal line. Each can limit the other and they do not automatically find alignment. A bridging oval represents common ground to resolve conflicts. It takes discipline to build an intentional bridge between the two, but it is in this bridging zone that the diagram emphasizes a key role for designers.

Note that the horizontal line implies a downward direction or an upward direction.

A downward motion indicates that both sides, through direct negotiations, have seen fit to compromise their stated values to a moderate degree. Some form of this kind of negotiation is common. But if the compromises descend further, the issue might devolve into a court battle, where for both sides, the risk of losing big greatly increases. Anything done to encourage early settlements tends to minimize environmental damage and accommodate much of the stated development need.

An upward motion in the diagram implies each side has found their aspirations have not only been met but exceeded. The result is a rare win-win outcome. It happens, and when it does, it is attributed to a *new idea* that neither side had ever considered. That's creative thinking, and that's the role of the design professions.

Whenever this simple diagram was used to orient students and young professionals to the work before them—whether it was in the early days of JJR or in recent sessions with current students—they got it. The prospects of working with others to foster creative dialogue toward finding the proper fit was enormous motivation. The students and young professionals of the time were quick to realize they were developing creative design tools for a role much more strategic than they had first realized.

The Advocate Role

Anyone working at the center of this diagram as a planning/design professional is and must be an advocate of *wise preservation policy* and *wise development policy*. Increasingly, development initiatives need to be more environmentally resilient, sustainable, and even regenerative. By working at both ends of the spectrum, greater wisdom is being sought by finding the *most fitting balance* integrating the two interests. It is a challenging task that calls for a deliberate, comprehensive planning/design process.

The advocate role at either end of the spectrum is different. It is aimed at *giving voice to and standing guard over* the stated values and aspirations of each end. I can attest to the importance of this advocacy role. In one case, a group of local citizens tied themselves to trees to halt further destruction of a revered park by the construction of a highway. In another case, as residents of a neighborhood were on the verge of selling out to a developer who planned to build a strip development shopping center, a social worker asked the residents at the last minute whether they were sure they wanted to sell. In both instances, an opportunity was created for wiser, more balanced thinking, resulting in solutions that far exceeded expectations.

But the advocate role is especially complex since it borders on *activism* without clear boundaries. In my planning and design experience, preservation or development advocacy is a powerful force when coupled with a problem-solving process. Advocacy, which is not part of a problem-solving process, seems to be different. On its own, advocacy promotes interests and causes. Short of taking strong actions, such as demonstrations, advocacy can teeter into activism, becoming an important societal alarm, as in global warming.

The Other Parts of the Diagram

The potential conflict. Fig. 12 illustrates two conflicting interests: stated preservation values and development values. Both are likely to generate intense advocacy. Note the distance between them; it symbolizes the difficulty of finding common ground. The column below each interest provides a few typical kinds of preservation standards or types of development initiatives that can trigger a public problem-solving process.

The Center. Here the diagram focuses on two key elements. The problem-solving arena at the center and the column below it shows samples of available resolution mechanisms such as science and technology, legislation, and mediation. For the design professions, these two elements comprise the engine that drives the diagram's overall message of creative problem-solving. If the *right ideas* can be found at the right time

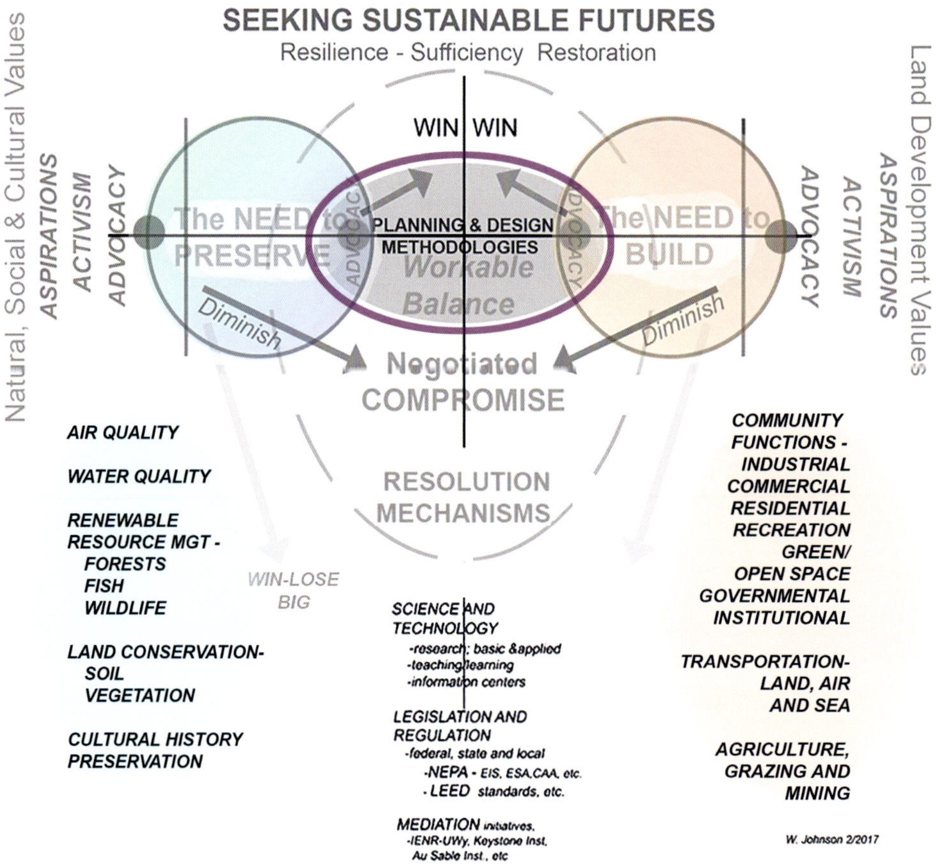

it can change a bleak outlook to a surprise success. To find such ideas takes an unusual level of process leadership, professional design skill, and confidence.

FIG. 12: The advocacy ends of the two conflicting interests — preservation and development — and the center problem-solving arena.

The Basic Equation for Our Current and Future Challenges

The original intention of illustrating the serious conflict between people and the earth was to alert emerging professionals in the design fields to the nature of the problem and the potential creative role they could play. Environmental issues circa 1960 were just beginning to take on the importance they deserved. The diagram was meant to inspire excellence as well as encourage participation and innovation.

The Basic Equation message is not only still relevant; it has become more important than ever. A sharper focus on conflict resolution mechanisms increases its usefulness.

What are the new circumstances that need to be recognized? Primarily, they relate to scientific and technological advances and undeniable global evidence of irreversible damage.

The "People–Place" challenge remains today, accompanied by noticeable shifts in the last 60 years.

A major reason is that the urgency of finding a fit between people and place has accelerated because of the growing importance of living sustainably. The Basic Equation is rooted in the notion of stewardship of our lands and resources. As Wendell Berry put it so eloquently in 1977, "But the care of the earth is our most ancient and most worthy and, after all, our most pleasing responsibility. To cherish what remains of it, and to foster its renewal, is our only legitimate hope."[11] Protecting our natural and cultural assets is just as important, sometimes perhaps more so, than the need to build. Shaping the future of our communities involves a combination of policy, project, and programmatic alignment that leans on various disciplinary focuses. Sustainable design, for instance, may have more of a project focus; integrating sustainability, on the other hand, is likely to find its way into policy discussions.

FIG. 13: The three legs of the "Sustainability Stool".

With the broad acceptance of sustainability as a common goal, the People–Place Equation now encompasses a third factor: "Prosperity." This equation has often been called the "Equity–Ecology–Economy" triad[12] or the three legs of the "Sustainability Stool."

Prosperity is centered on the economic wellbeing of a community and looks at economic impacts beyond growth and profits. It includes important quantitative and qualitative outcomes such as employment creation, innovation, community redevelopment, and reinvestment. Finding an appropriate balance among the three factors can lead to win-win outcomes. A compromise in any one factor can diminish long-term community strength.

More importantly, the People–Place–Prosperity paradigm of sustainability is not an accounting system like those used in businesses and data reports. Rather, it is a holistic framework for tracking, understanding, and managing the systemic effects of human activity.

A second shift is evidenced in the recognition of "Equity." Since the civil rights movements of the 1960s, we appear to be reaching new social tipping points. Globally, there is a groundswell of effort to support access to opportunity. The equity lens thus recenters issues of race, disability, income, and age, among others, in the Basic Equation.

As such, the People element is no longer seen as a homogeneous whole. Instead, we are called to contemplate questions such as these:

- Who are the historically under-served and under-represented populations?
- How are we engaging them? What are their barriers to access and participation?
- How might our professional practice and recommendations thoughtfully address the different perspectives that emerge in each process?
- What are the potential impacts of our planning and design work across various populations?
- How can we manage the tradeoffs and seek fairness for all participants?

Third, there has been a *greater mindfulness of the long-term view* in recent decades. At its heart, the Basic Equation is a *blending of long-term (aspirations) with short-term reality (pragmatism)*. A long-term Vision guides short-term decisions. In turn, short-term insights can provide feedback to sharpen a Vision.

In planning and design, there have been shifts toward new techniques and approaches that balance long-term environmental concerns with short-term development needs. Coastal protection, for instance, has seen the adoption of "softer" resiliency approaches like living shorelines in response to changing sea and lake levels in populated communities.

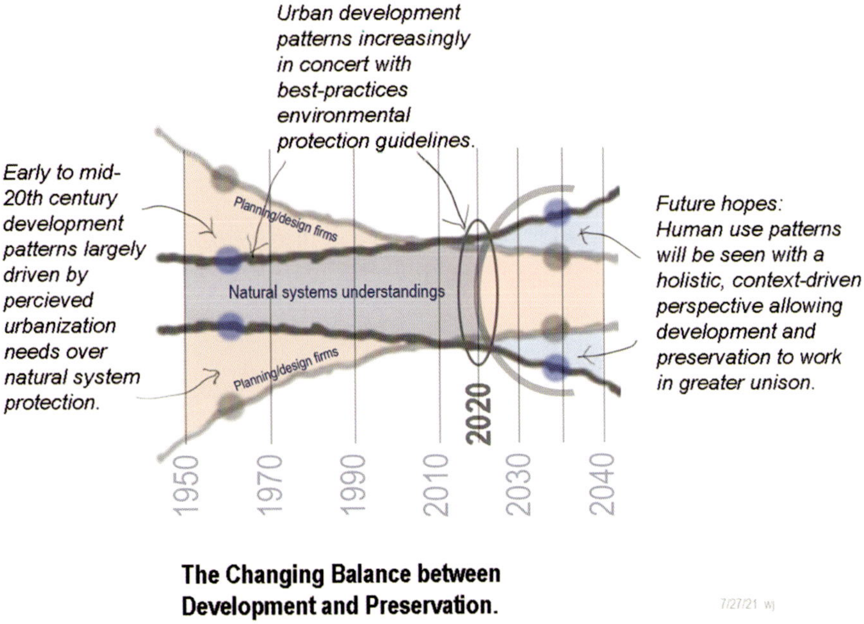

FIG. 14: Shifts in the preservation-development balance over the last six decades.

Similarly, passive design strategies for buildings seek to reduce energy consumption by optimizing the use of natural sources of heating, cooling, and ventilation, and by minimizing dependency on mechanical systems.[13] Green infrastructure, which encompasses green stormwater management systems, park systems and urban forests, constructed wetlands, green streets, and green roofs, also demonstrates the growing attention to the long-term view.

Over the last 60 years, there has been a fundamental change in the balance between development and preservation.[14] While early to mid-20th century, development patterns have been largely driven by perceived growth and urbanization needs over natural systems protection, broader environmental awareness and natural systems understandings have gained strength steadily. Urbanization patterns, especially in more populated metropolitan areas from Toronto to Tokyo, are increasingly in concert with environmental best practices guidelines.

At the same time, there are still strides to be made and realities to reckon with. Sprawling growth, environmental degradation, and stretched planning and resource capacities remain. Yet the hope, as shared by many, is for development and preservation to work in greater unison. In finding the sustainable fit and long-term balance we seek, we now turn to three basic understandings essential to any land planning professional entering the practice: knowing the "Playing Field," building early "Leverage," and understanding the great scale range in "The Big Canvas."

CHAPTER TWO

UNDERSTANDINGS

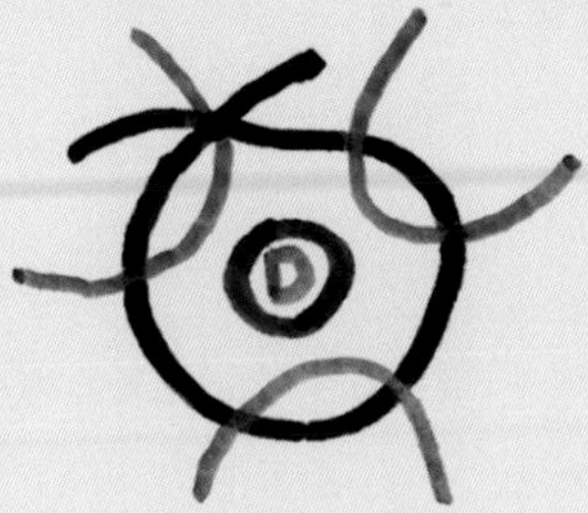

THE PLAYING FIELD

The Multidisciplinary Team Approach

Knowing one's "Playing Field" begins to tell the story of when and how one joins a game. Community planning is both an art and a science, dealing with increasingly complex issues. Considering the many interests involved, from community members and interest groups, to planning and design professionals as well as policymakers, it suggests that a multidisciplinary way of thinking is essential. Inputs coming from one area of understanding build on those from other areas; this interplay of insights leads to the creative dialogue we seek.

THE PLAYING FIELD

When I chose a career in landscape architecture, it felt essential to me to know the "Playing Field"—the learning and working context of how landscape architecture relates to allied fields and professions. Any quality professional degree program, undergraduate or graduate, will contain some version of that. However, there seems to be chronic confusion about the identity of landscape architecture. This leads to several persistent concerns:

- First, that young professionals might not have a clear understanding of the full range of distinctively different career choices *within* the design discipline.
- Second, landscape architects need to know that it is a *design-centered* discipline with *strong edges overlapping with* the sciences and arts.
- Third, given landscape architecture's close interplay with the natural and social sciences, care should be taken to hold to the design discipline as the *primary identity* while trading ideas and collaborating with other disciplines.

Such concerns have been shared by working colleagues, leading to many heated discussions about identity—and leading in turn to many napkin-drawn diagrams aimed at defining professional identity more clearly. One message became loud and clear—whatever career choice might be made, assembling and working in *interdisciplinary teams would mark their future*.

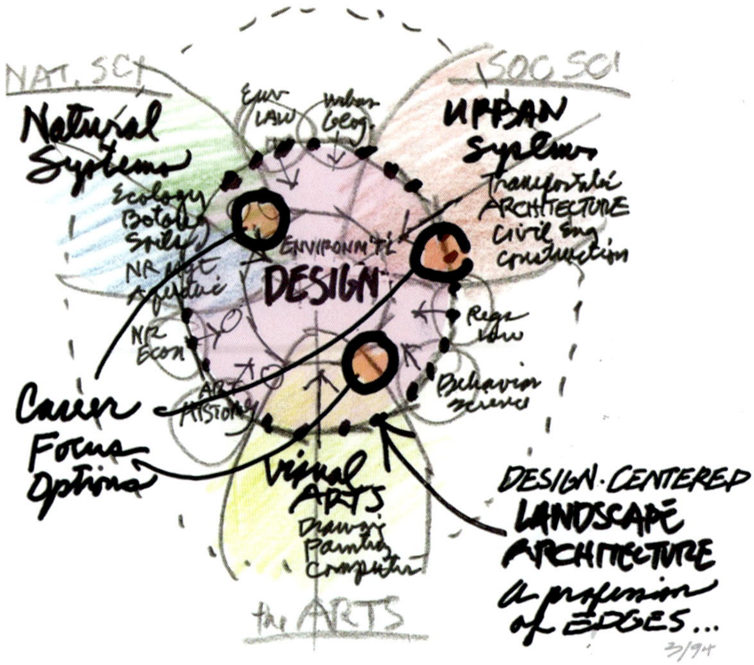

FIG. 15: An early napkin sketch of the Playing Field.

Another napkin sketch is shown here in Fig. 15.

It illustrates a design-centered circle surrounded by natural systems, urban systems, and the visual arts. Three small focus points represent different choices, like a choice to work in concert with natural resource disciplines, or to emphasize collaborations with urban designers and architects/engineers, or to concentrate on form-based solutions with artists/sculptors.

Diagrams of this kind are used often in lectures and presentations and have been refined over time. Fig. 16 is a refined version of the original sketch on a napkin.

The Current and Future Playing Field for Design and Allied Professionals

Although concern about identity for the landscape architect is less of an issue today, the message about a life of teamwork is as relevant as ever.

FIG. 16: A refined diagram of the Playing Field showing the multidisciplinary and interdisciplinary ways of working.

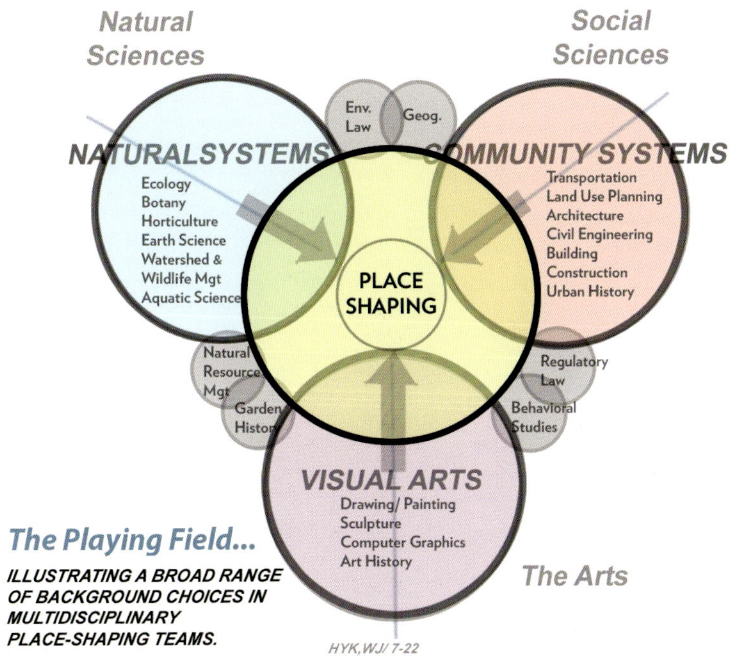

The diagram has interdependency written all over it. But a new dimension has been emerging. It is about learning to foster, encourage, and support inspired team leadership throughout a problem-solving process. To be an effective facilitator, one needs skills in creating space for meaningful participation and establishing shared understandings toward a common goal. Often, there is a vacuum of the kind of leadership that fosters the search for ideas, champions a fitting idea when found, and sustains creative energy. Landscape architects and other planning and design professionals have an opportunity to seize this role.

In the place shaping and place making professions, the search for ideas is the primary focus. If ideas of the right kind found at the right time can bring positive change, then a well-facilitated, interdisciplinary team has much to offer. There are strengths we can draw on from different backgrounds, and it is important to lean into the community insights, talents, and assets at hand. That seems to be a point well worth emphasizing to encourage young design professionals entering the game. Our

FIG. 17: Facilitating a multidisciplinary and interdisciplinary workshop with community leaders.

friends at the Project for Public Spaces sum this up so well: "Look for partners" and remember, "the community is the expert."[15]

Our hope is that now, and in the future, *all professionals* will recognize that different problems benefit from different approaches. In some cases, the architectural solution works hand in glove with landscape design. In others, the systems approach in landscape planning reveals the key, overarching strategy to define smaller architectural moves thereafter. More notably, the process of place shaping and community building draws on a broad range of background choices. The creative problem-solving role is one of them. Others include development, implementation, policy and advocacy, environmental protection and restoration, and cultural and historical stewardship.

The beauty of the team approach is its richness. Within the creative problem-solving roles, we bring diverse training, perspectives, and values to the table. Teams also bring a range of understandings across age, gender, color, culture, and faith. Bridging those differences is hard, and sometimes we don't, but when peppered with a generous dose of openness, curiosity, and good humor, we are nudged closer to finding common ground and more gratifying outcomes.

Above all, the success of a team approach lies not only in the internal team dynamics but also hinges on how the team engages the people and cultures of a place. What are their stories? What are their needs, dreams, and aspirations? What are their concerns? Why are these important? How would they like their community to feel?

In short, this might mean leaving the "expertise" at the door. Perhaps go by first names, drop the titles, and start every dialogue on a clean slate. We are not necessarily there to inform but to learn. The hope is to move from "you and me" to "us and we."

EARLY, EARLY, EARLY

Impact Increases with Early Involvement

This reminder icon about being "Early" is all about common sense. It was first used to encourage those working to bring forth natural and cultural resource preservation ideas. Even though their reasoning might be sound and their ideas achievable, if they express them too late it can be difficult to work them into the emerging concepts of fixed building form. So, getting ideas early makes all kinds of good sense. Now, it is broader than that. It suggests that the design process itself, by its iterative nature, can be geared to an "early, early, early" or a "heads up" format. No more "too lates."

EARLY, EARLY, EARLY

The reminder to become involved early in the game was first a response to a quirky relationship in the 1950s and 1960s between landscape architects and those in related professions: architecture, planning, and engineering. It was generally understood that trees, shrubs, and flowers were final stage features of a building program. So, the landscape architect would be called in accordingly, and they tended to accept a late-stage role. It became a pattern.

The more considered logic was 180 degrees different. For instance, the Vision for downtown resurgence in Holland, Michigan, that was described in the introduction was preceded by a brief outline of principles to work by. It was done early to assure that understandings were clear before planning complexities increased and clouded the view.

The following is a summary of the understandings among those who gathered to work together:

- First was an *alliance of key leaders*, where public and private partnerships were conceived.
  - › Strategic entrepreneurship was a norm.
  - › Creative philanthropy was encouraged.
  - › There was a concept of "patient capital" where somebody could contribute capital and be willing to wait 10 years for the return.
- Second was being *Vision-centered*.
  - › Seeking and finding inspiration from the situation at hand.
  - › Keeping a Vision active, and, once found, refreshed.

  › Understanding the short term when shaping the long term.
  › Seeking innovation where new ideas are encouraged.
- Third, it was *values* based.
  › Recognizing different and shared values and seeking common ground.
  › Honoring other people's views in creating dialogue.
  › Sustaining the values and principles as evaluation lenses for decision-making.
- Fourth, a "First Things First" reality.
  › A certain kind of practicality unique to Dutch heritage.
  › Assuring that key sites for the future are in friendly hands.
- And finally, *working smart*.
  › Energized by the search for ideas.
  › Fostering strong relationships for making things happen in service to the common good.

Of such familiar change agents as money, influence, regulations, and ideas, the most penetrating and enduring is so often the *power of an idea*. We enjoyed reminding each other that *ideas of the right kind at the right time can change things beyond our expectations*. What a great reminder that was!

From its beginning, the JJR firm lived by the principle of getting in there early, whether it was through demonstrated issue awareness, proposal making, or contract agreements. In doing so, we were able to foster key collaboration understandings and keen context awareness to shape countless building and engineering projects. It was an important message about influence and leverage—the icon was meant to be a reminder.

Early in the design process when a *Vision search* is beginning, analyses of various kinds are underway, and evaluation criteria are forming, there are placemaking principles at work. There are four that I have found to be most revealing:

› Stay centered on a Vision.
› Know the place and the people.
› Build ideas with others.
› Think Framework.

First, think in contextual references beginning with *centering on a Vision*, and then jointly building a commonly held and inspirational description of an intended future ... excitement about an idea and the beginnings of what would be called a Vision. In the Vision-building process, we need to learn how to keep it working even as other phases of development/design are underway. "Keep the Vision on the table" is an essential reminder.

Second, commit to a process of truly getting to know the place one is working with, in physical, cultural, and historical terms. Know the people who live, work, and play in that place. The intent is to build deep understandings, particularly where change is intended. These studies are the primary source of ideas that fit.

Third, build ideas *with* others. Work together and frame spirited discussions on how ideas are found.

Lastly, this reminder ... keep thinking *Framework*.

See the whole as you work with the parts—a valuable principle.

Early involvement enables early understandings, opportunities, and key place shaping principles to influence project outcomes. Early leverage also calls for the ability to exercise *process leadership*. This understanding of leadership is distinct from the traits that define a leader. It shifts the focus from the individual to the interaction between the team and the client, and from given characteristics to process qualities that can be observed, learned, and trained.[16]

To be early implies the importance of early interactions that invite others to come along on the journey. It is not always about being at the front or being the one with all the answers or making the decisions. On the contrary, it suggests that the role of the leader of a process is to listen, learn, facilitate, support, and guide—often in the background.

Being early is also about asking good questions, whether to seek clarification of what is meant and intended or to encourage new wonderings and ways of seeing. In enabling others to "see more" early on, we begin to plant the seeds for discovery, strategy, and form.

Lastly, being early involves giving thought and intention to create conditions for the team to succeed.[17] Do we have a clear, compelling direction to engage and energize the team? Do we have the right mix and

FIG. 18: Building ideas with others early in the process.

number of members to complement each other? Do we have the right supports in place to enable team effectiveness? How are we building shared understanding and appreciation to encourage cooperation and communication?

Above all, to be early implies being able and willing to play a lead role in directing attention to Vision and context considerations before such opportunities slip by. This context-centered mindset is a key principle we will turn to next in "The Big Canvas."

FIG. 19: Visioning as a process.

Visioning as a Process, by William Johnson

"A Vision is not meant to be precise, but rather directional in nature. Its purpose is to help prioritize future occurrences and opportunities so that, for example, when an underutilized defunct Downtown property suddenly becomes available, it is relatively easy to refer to the Vision and have a good sense of what belongs (and what does not) and how development concepts might be shaped to best fit the property into the overall Vision."

The visioning process is a logical progression of steps which taken together will establish the future goals and direction for a community. This diagram was devised by William Johnson to graphically define the process.

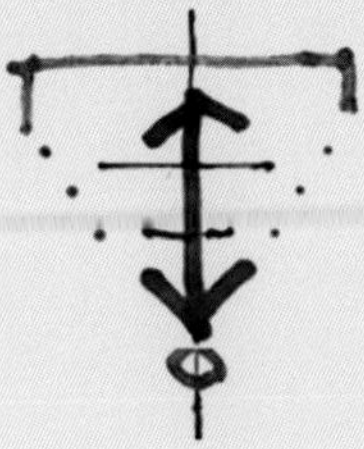

THE BIG CANVAS

Learning to be Adept at Great Scale Changes

"The Big Canvas" icon is a reminder to those involved with community building that different environmental scales or urban scales are always at work—sometimes dramatically so (like a neighborhood creek to a river watershed). A shift in scale can be disconcerting, but it's part of the territory . . . they all interrelate. Note how the icon features a vertical arrow connecting the small with the large. This is the beginning of Framework Thinking in which all the parts and pieces are seen in the context of the whole.

THE BIG CANVAS

Among the most familiar set of sister disciplines (planning, urban design, architecture, and engineering), landscape architecture is the one with a curriculum primarily based on natural systems as core elements. Landscape architects' learning is characterized by a broad understanding of the ecosystem and at an extensive scale that transcends individual buildings. Accordingly, their design outlook follows suit with a broad-based approach to development form, wherein the search for context understandings is fundamental.

In a memorable brainstorming session with Professor Hideo Sasaki in grad school, he quietly said to us, "There are no scale limitations to design—if you can assess the circumstances at play for a residential garden, you can do the same for a coastal development strategy." Heady talk. I will never forget it. The realization of that principle came up several times in my first five years in practice as a founding partner of JJR. I do not remember ever being ill at ease with the great scale ranges we experienced in project assignments.

For instance, early in the 1960s in our office there were several design projects of a specific site-scale, like a residence or an office building. We worked out a site design solution for each accordingly and these projects fit easily on a typical medium-sized worktable.

At the same time, we had an assessment of the natural resource features of the entire upper peninsula of Michigan which was hung nearby on a floor-to-ceiling wall. The task was to see whether the many priceless

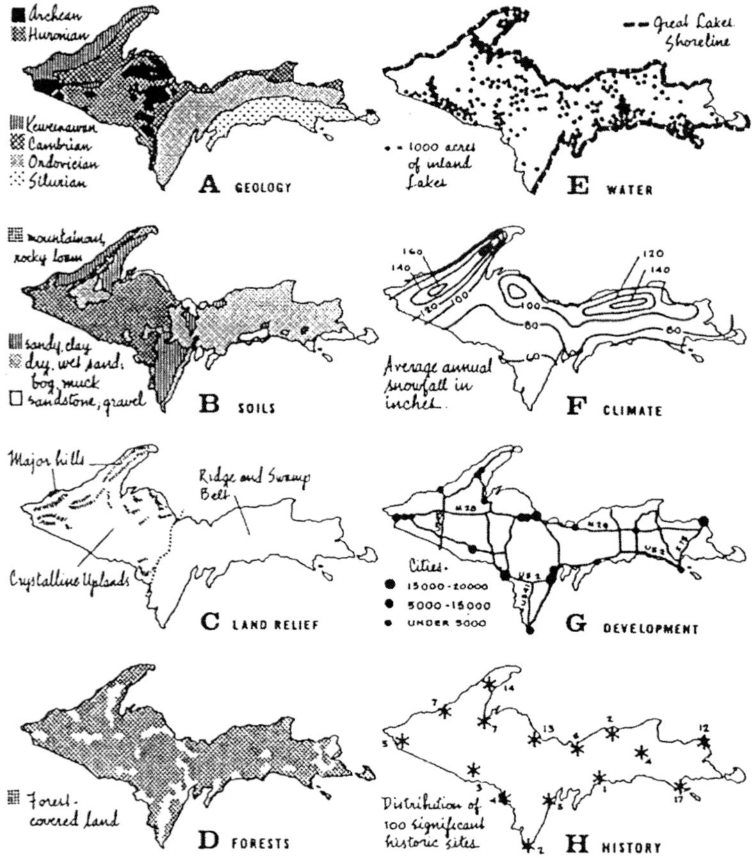

FIG. 20: Guidelines for tourism in the Upper Peninsula, Michigan (c. 1966), completed in collaboration with Uel Blank and Clare Gunn. The series of plans from the entire Upper Peninsula to a region, and a waterfront downtown in Menominee demonstrate how there were no limits to scale in planning/design in the 'Framework' approach.

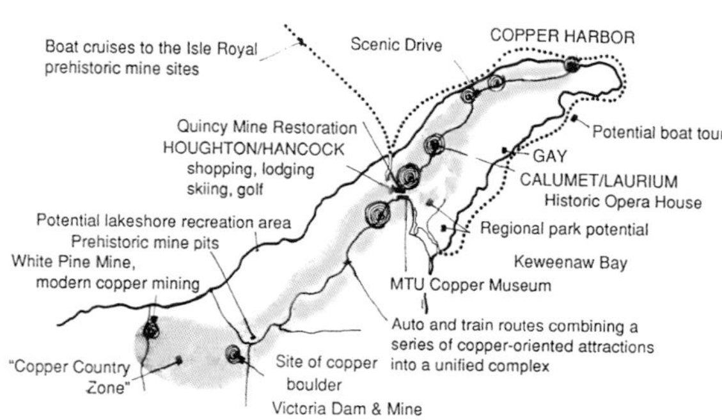

natural features could help to revive the region's tourism industry without endangering the quality of the features themselves. A regional tourism strategy was eventually worked out and submitted to the state.

As such, on any workday morning, one could spend time at a worktable on a two-acre site plan, then turn around for afternoon work on a sixteen-thousand-square-mile natural resource preservation strategy of a completely different scale on the wall. To us, the shifts between the two scales were seamless. Such scale variations were part of our everyday practice throughout the 50-year history of JJR.

It suggested an important role for such broadly based design types, that is, a design-oriented bridging discipline between the natural and cultural sciences and the building professions (architecture, engineering). It implied the need to be there early in the problem-solving process and the willingness and know-how to take the lead as needed.

Keeping the Big Canvas in View

In the 60 years since first urging young planners and designers to become adept at great differentials of scale, much has happened along those lines. In general, urban designers and landscape architects, in concert with architects and engineers, have learned the importance of knowing how to work with context in mind. There have been great strides in environmentally sensitive project solutions. They are increasingly involved early and are willing to take leads in the process as needed.

But certain chronic challenges persist. One is resistance to the Big Canvas principle. It's simply human nature: We seem to be built to predominantly hear one song and mostly narrow sets of details. We seem to be fascinated with where the decisions are forming at the expense of allowing the guiding force of knowing and honoring the larger context findings.

The Big Canvas is a gentle reminder that multiple perspectives from afar and up-close offer a fuller picture of a community's needs, conditions, and opportunities. This agility to slide across manifold scales from the context to the site and from the functions to the connecting systems essentially constitute a *"zoom in"* Framework.[18] In many ways this is much like Google Earth or GIS functions that enable us to toggle seamlessly between the regional viewpoint emphasizing patterns of uses, linkages, and forms, and a building-scale perspective in a community.

Cultivating the ability to zoom also suggests the possibility of *avoiding a bifurcated world of extremes—situational or structural, specific or contextual*. Zooming across the Big Canvas thus allows us to remain grounded in realities. What are the unique elements of a site or a case study? What broader themes or principles can be gleaned?

Extra care is called for in planning and development where community, economic, and environmental implications abound. Often, politically expedient initiatives to achieve short-term effects may seem successful. Yet, if they are not coherent and well thought through, such measures may come at the cost of public trust and confidence, and long-term decline and disinvestment.

Zooming in therefore also happens across temporal scales, especially in the context of the Basic Equation today. What are the environmental constraints and values? What are the regulatory details? How could the project be phased in? What are the near-term tradeoffs and the long-term impacts?

By clarifying the relationship between the big picture context, the key ideas, and the actionable first moves, this approach helps to set goals in motion with a clear order of operations, priorities, and assignment of roles for early implementation. When stakeholders can see immediate results, and small wins match broad Visions, it demonstrates feasibility.

The intent of *Framework Thinking* is to *blend principles and realities, aspirations and pragmatism*. It is an appeal to linger just a little longer to see more within the Big Canvas and discover the most fitting idea before delving into the details.

CHAPTER THREE

PROCESS

THE SEARCH

Energizing an Iterative, Problem-Solving Process

"The Search" icon describes the exploratory way we have learned to shape community. It is an iterative, analytical, and creative problem-solving process that has been practiced, taught, and proven effective throughout my 60-plus years of practice. Often referred to as the "Design Process," it is a guide to steps along the way toward planning and implementing perceived needs. There are many variations, but common to all are deliberate efforts to understand the need, the place, and the people involved, to set aside time for creative plan-making, and to lay out a concluding decision-making path. The special skill of participating in and leading the Search is an essential ingredient of Framework Thinking.

THE SEARCH

The JJR approach to planning and design was an intriguing mix of order and spontaneity. Often, our potential clients would ask ... *How do you work? How do you want us involved?* We would try to describe how we assessed the process priorities, what we were after, and how we worked to get it done. We would further explain that during the early part of the design process, there were ways we worked to bring out the essence of where the preferred Vision would begin to form and where the design form would most likely show itself.

Due to clients' great interest in being involved, we discovered a new dimension to our services and invited client groups in with open arms. We wanted our client groups (mostly institutional) to not only feel welcome but also to be energized by our studio setting. We found that in our studio, people relaxed and opened up more easily to a dialogue. It allowed us to create a familiar setting for sketching displays and presentations when the Vision search was beginning, analytics of various kinds were underway, and placemaking principles were forming. We delighted in this process of discovery!

Clients would come into the office to enjoy the discourse of IDEA discovery. In the early days at JJR, we often referred to this as the *"Ways of Working."* It was an important term to us since we felt that the way we generated a dialogue was as important as the dialogue itself.

The physical organization of our office was helpful. We designed a two-level open forum just for this kind of creative engagement in our

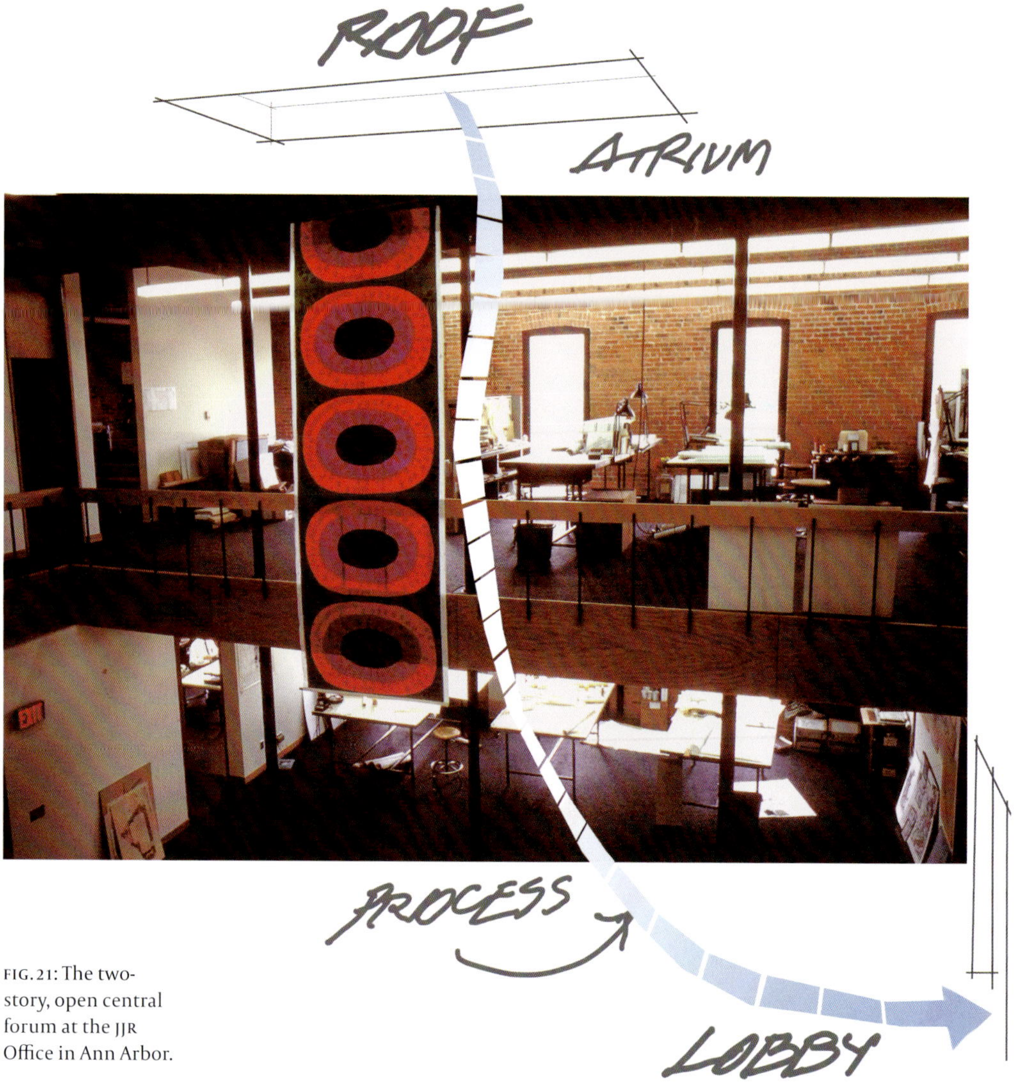

FIG. 21: The two-story, open central forum at the JJR Office in Ann Arbor.

building on Main Street in Ann Arbor. It enabled those on the upper floor to look down on projects and hear the discussions. The two-story walls were left blank, allowing us to tack up sketches and discussion notes. It was a perfect kind of place to gather for casual meetings and seminars; its openness induced feelings of trust.

When such intentional gathering places are part of the design process, it makes it easy to trade ideas. You go to the wall and draw something on it. Then you throw a plan on the table and the group gathers around it to figure out better ways to make things work. Simple conversations lead to unexpected ideas, some of which prevail to the final concept. It's just an exciting, enjoyable way of working.

We simply called it the "Design Process."

At that time, there was a profession-wide debate on the distinctions between Planning and Design. "Design-only" proponents argued that Planning was not a Design discipline, but a "policy-oriented" discipline with broader, community-building outcomes. Our convictions at JJR were that in the interest of problem-solving and spatial continuity, the term "Planning" was best under the rubric of "Design." It was and still is a term that meant a scale of thinking and analysis extending beyond the limits of a building at an architectural scale, to consider the site, the context, and sometimes the region. But many of my colleagues disagreed, continuing to refer to the early due diligence as "analysis paralysis." The true Design act seemed reserved for distinctive physical form, referring to it as the "Built Landscape." This separation of the Planning and Design terms, each with its own definition, has persisted through the years, and that significantly weakens the broader Framework approach discussed in this book.

Broad to Narrow Process Continuity—Seek the Integration of Planning, Design, and Build

As JJR grew, we continued to follow our deliberate approach to the Process, leaving a good deal of room for spontaneity. Our assignments kept broadening in scale and variety; they included campus planning for

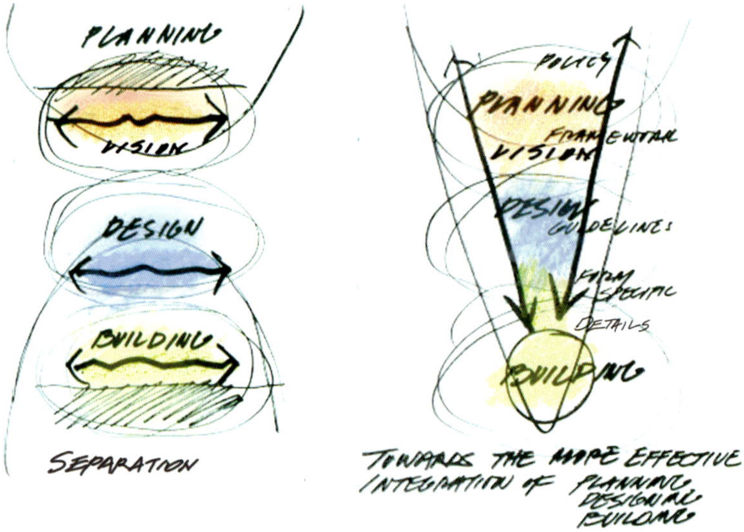

Fig.22: Design process separating *vs* integrating Planning and Design.

academic and corporate institutions, state and federal highway location studies, natural resource and historic preservation studies, downtown revitalization projects, and community parks and recreation systems. They were all multi-layered ... more complex than expected, each calling for the deliberate process we were offering.

We learned that the early search for context understandings and the process of building a Vision could be time-consuming, often beyond reason. To be effective, we needed to formulate our findings quickly. We worked hard to make Vision statements and supportive diagram(s) brief, clear, and intriguing. Loose early versions were shared to invite the team and various interest groups into further dialogue and to fuel greater creativity for the discovery process.

- Early in the process, while the assessment of the objectives and the circumstances at hand were underway, *Vision-building discussions* began. It was a creative dialogue among all stakeholders, triggered by the "easy graphic" portrayals of ideas that were described earlier.

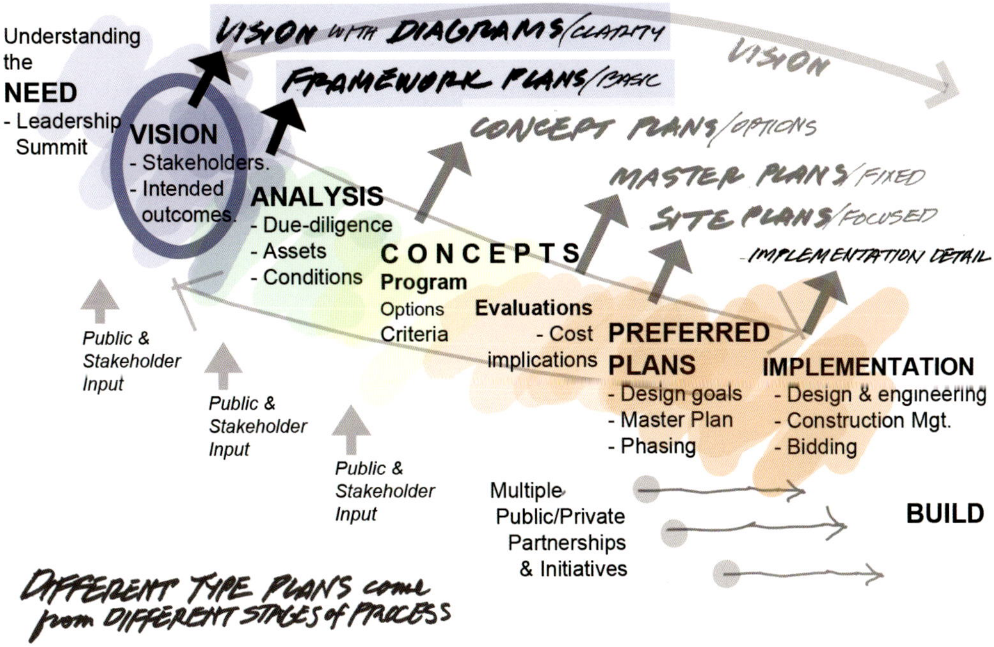

FIG. 23: Different plans come from different stages of the Planning-Design process.

- A preferred Vision and a supportive diagram emerged from these discussions, which we often referred to as *the Bones*. We later called it a *Framework plan*. It expressed a *basic direction* for the long-term future.
- Ideas abounded, which led to the framing of *Alternative Concepts*. The number varied because they came from a broad array of interests.
- A set of *Evaluation Criteria* was resolved and applied. Meant to assess the tradeoffs, strengths, and weaknesses of different futures, these plans became quite site specific and were subject to cost evaluations and new levels of detail. Such evaluations usually narrowed the choice to two or three workable long-term *Concept plans*.
- A final summary plan was drawn up, keeping the variables but providing design detail for the First Phase. Most planners referred to it as a *Master Plan*. It differs from the earlier Framework plan. The Framework plan carefully outlines the basic Bones of future direction without prescribing detail, so that the Vision it represents will be an enduring record of the intended dream. The Master Plan and its later revisions describe the plan in site-specific architectural detail.

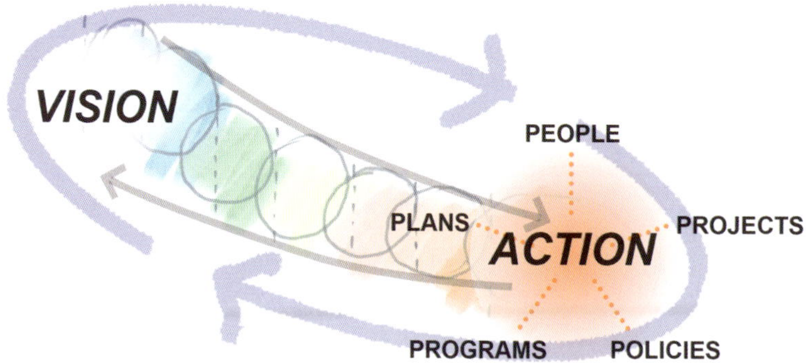

FIG. 24: Combination of people, plans, projects, programs, and policies grounded in robust analytics and due diligence needed to drive a Vision to action (credits: Har Ye Kan).

This sequence of deliberate problem solving can apply to any scale of development need, but it is often on the broader side; it can apply to a community as a whole or to a sizable portion of a community such as a downtown, a particular gateway corridor, or a neighborhood. The scale of time in mind is long-term, say 10 to 20 years or more. There will be many short-term initiatives arising along the way within the context of the overall Process.

Besides a "building" oriented outcome, the more immediate, incremental steps can also be realized through programs, policies, partnerships, and additional planning, such as fleshing out the Visions in subarea plans, development standards, and capital and operational budgets. Who the client is can likewise shape approaches to realizing development and conservation. Working for a private developer is not the same as working for a nonprofit organization or a local government. There is a need for both the catalyst project and the right policies in place, and an embedded culture carrying the long-term Vision to achieve the intended goals. For instance, stream and prairie restorations in a conservation community development are projects; tree planting and green infrastructure are best practices; and historic preservation design guidelines are policy choices.

Weak Points in the Design Process

For project-oriented outcomes, most architects and planners who work through the kind of process we speak of here do it well. But they do not always keep the earlier Vision relevant as the process becomes more focused on detailed site and building form. Midway through the Design Process, there is a tendency for the Vision to weaken due to a shift of mindsets from those skilled at the Visionary end to those motivated to get it built. This point of weakness is a serious issue.

The two mindsets are different and do not mix easily. It is rare for one person to embody both. Therefore, continuity is critical as a project moves from one stage to the next. It takes persistence and the wherewithal and willingness to carry the Vision forward and work through challenges. Without determined local leadership to bridge the potential gap, the Process could break apart into two pieces. What may have first emerged as a transformational Vision then runs the risk of being set aside or undermined by complex pragmatic issues, yielding more prosaic outcomes.

The notion of "transformational" and "transactional" leadership and how the two need to be combined can be traced to Goodwin's *Leadership in Turbulent Times*. In her analysis of four American presidents—Abraham Lincoln, Theodore Roosevelt, Franklin D. Roosevelt, and Lyndon B. Johnson—she noted:

> *Among the many variants of leadership, scholars have sought to identify two seemingly antithetical types—transactional, by far the more common, and transformational. Transactional leaders operate pragmatically. They appeal to the self-interest of their followers, using quid pro quos, bargains, trades and rewards to solicit support and influence the behavior of their followers. Transformational leaders inspire followers to identify with something larger than themselves—the organization, the community, the region, the country—and finally, to the more abstract identification with the ideals of that country. Such leaders call for sacrifice in the pursuit of moral principles and higher goals, validating such altruisms by*

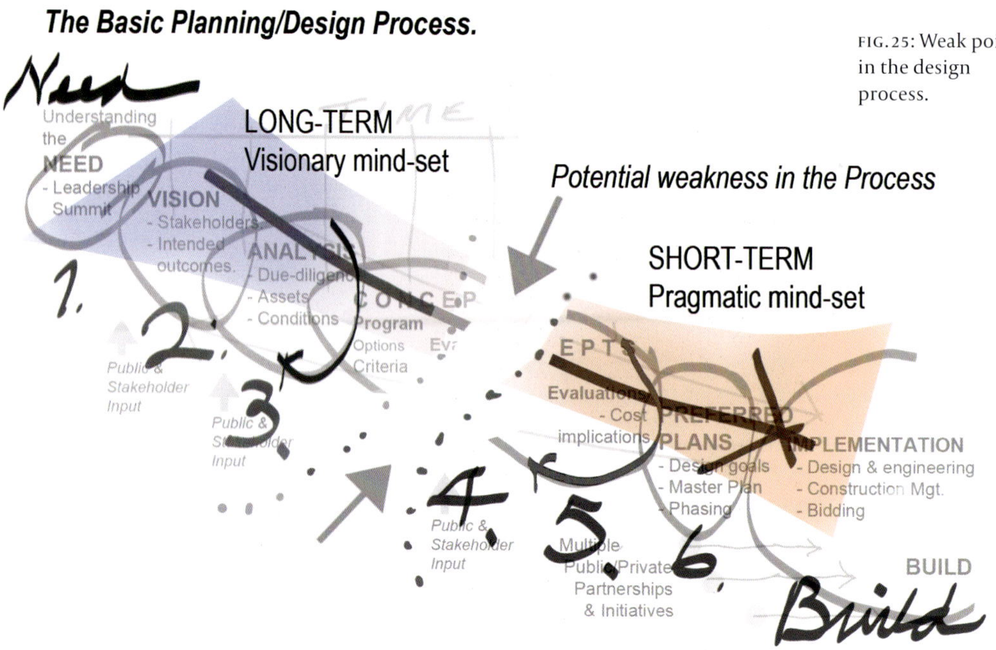

FIG. 25: Weak points in the design process.

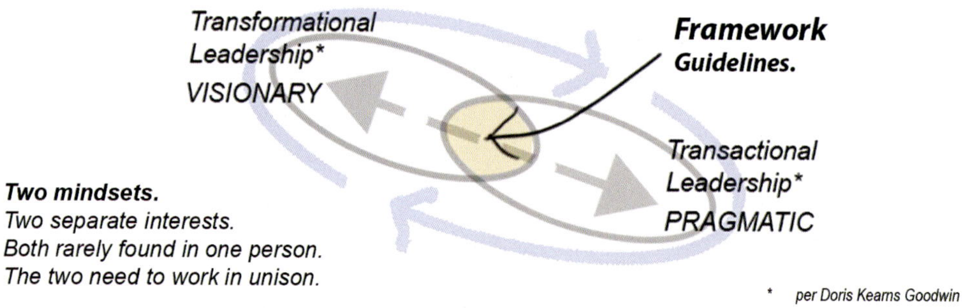

FIG. 26: Two mindsets with different interests to be bridged.

> *looking beyond the present moment to frame a future worth striving for ... For Lincoln, pragmatic, transactional strategies provided the nuts and bolts of principled, transformational leadership.*[19]

The same can be said for how a community Vision can be cast and what it takes for the Vision to be sustained. Today, more than ever, we need a strong design process and a Visionary approach to avoid "bits and pieces" patterns of urban development. To address this vulnerability, the next chapter, "Visions," will delve into how we can effectively cast and sustain a Vision across the design process.

VISIONS

Shaping an Enduring, Long-Term Vision

The "Visions" icon illustrates a capital "V" for the challenging task of Vision-building in the world of creative community planning. Producing the right kind of Vision at the right time may well be the most important product of the Design Process, since such a Vision can inspire, giving creative energy to subsequent levels of design detail. In short, the primary objective of the Process might be to prepare a commonly held Vision and strive to build out the most fitting place possible consistent with that Vision.

VISIONS

When I was in school at Michigan State/Harvard and in my early days at JJR, we didn't talk about Visions so much as we talked about Ideas. An "idea" was an important image to inspire. But the term "Vision" was not prominent in any way. It was about ideas.

A memorable moment for me took place in the drafting room at Harvard where I first met Pete Walker. We had been given a case study ... a problem needing to be solved. The case study involved each of us putting together a solution and presenting them to each other to discuss in a critique format. I was showing him the plan that I had come up with for a garden, telling him how it worked. When I finished, he commented that it had something good going, but it didn't hook together very well; there seemed to be a lot of nice bits and pieces but no particular idea about what I was after. It made me sit bolt upright.

I was chagrined. It was clear I was weak on having an overarching *Idea* or what later in my career could have also been called a *Vision*. I had no Vision that could have helped to put everything else into its proper place. I was left with a helter-skelter garden plan. It was an important learning moment with Pete being both my classmate and teacher. I appreciated his sharp mind as we later talked about different kinds of challenges in the design world.

Defining a Vision is elusive. At Michigan State I had an instructor, Professor Carl Gerlach, who taught us to find a prevailing Idea through art form. He would suggest that we put down an abstract pattern as you would in any kind of painting. We would then fit into that set of patterns our landscape materials—trees, terraces, shrubs—using the abstract form as a guide. But that did not sit well with me, because it was so arbitrary. I looked for other ways.

I recall the frequent use early on of the term "Concepts" along with Ideas. The term Visions came later, in the early JJR days. We were anxious to approach any design/planning project in a big picture way, making it quite natural to seek prevailing Ideas or Inspired Visions. We discovered early on that one of the immediate ways to energize the big picture perspective was the natural and cultural history of the site and community. Stakeholders value a deeper understanding of their home grounds and the highlights of their history. It builds trust in the professional team and is a major source for Visionary ideas.

Vision Building

Early in the Process, we learned to go to work at the earliest stages of building a Vision—not so much to shape a Vision but the process of *building* it. There is a way of going about it that includes the thinking of the entire team: community stakeholders, leaders, and professionals. In the end there needs to be a commonly held Vision for the future or its guiding force will not be found.

What? Why? How?

Discussions about the future brought up various concepts or Visions to be evaluated. Other discussions were aimed at developing a set of evaluation criteria. With this, the team can eventually choose the preferred Vision. Accordingly, the "what" and "how" can effectively be delivered. What about the "why"?

Why is a *commonly held* Vision needed? The most homespun way of talking about it might be to say a Vision is like a rudder on a ship. It may be one of the smallest pieces of a ship, but the rudder is the guiding force. A ship without a rudder is not going to go anywhere. I like to think about a Vision in that way ... small, but effective and powerful.

A Vision Realized

If you were to ask who creates the Vision, you could quickly say that it is all of us. So, early in the process, there ought to be a way in which the team gathers frequently to trade thoughts about hopes and dreams regarding the problems being faced. It includes a statement that is brief and to the point, accompanied by a diagram or two showing what it might look like. But it should not be so extensive that it could be confused with being a plan; it is only a basic direction.

At JJR, several Vision options usually emerged from discussions of that kind, calling for Evaluation Criteria developed along the way (a set of intended characteristics with the Vision in mind). In continuing discussions, the team began to assemble an inspirational statement and supporting diagrams. Leading this kind of dialogue takes skill and patience.

How an Effective Vision is Best Stated

Dialogue, or the exchange of ideas, is central to the Visioning process. It is important that the dialogue is easy and fluid. The way conversations are led is key to bringing an interesting and disarming spirit to the search. Openness and trust are important to shaping a Vision that will be commonly held. And it will prevail over time only to the degree most find it inspirational, easy to describe, and directly relevant. A quick sense of confidence in the process can be strengthened by building new ideas around existing attributes that the community already has going for it. A Vision statement should *inspire*. It should suggest a future that seems to fit the tangible circumstances at hand while at the same time it dares to describe a prospect that rises above the daily grind of "nuts and bolts."

The Vision statement can be expressed in written and graphic terms, but both need to be brief, succinct, and highly generalized. This succinct

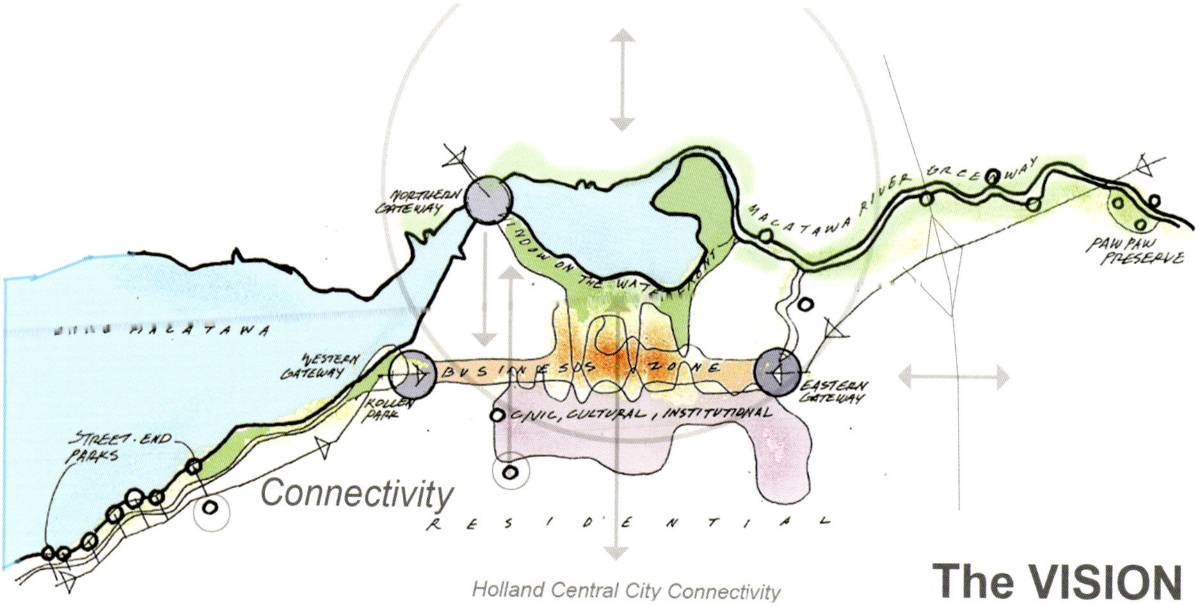

FIG. 27: The Downtown Holland Vision diagram.

1989 Holland Downtown Vision statement, also shared earlier in the book, is a good example.

> *A New Kind of Destination Downtown.*
> *A PLACE of distinction, where quality shops and residential life co-mingle, where campus functions blend with the urban center, where tiny green places provide respite, where waterfronts are lined with greenways and walkability is a priority. This is the spirit of the kind of Downtown we seek.*

Keep It on The Table

At JJR, we felt it was a major achievement to build a commonly held Vision—a solid, inspiring direction. But there is a shift of mindsets now; the issues at hand are more narrowly focused on detailed design, engineering, and cost considerations. *This is a major shift from those who think broadly—visionaries—to those who think narrowly—pragmatists.* Both are essential but the two do not mix easily. For the design process at this stage, continuity is critical. Finding leaders who can bridge the two is a key step.

Here is the point where the commonly held Vision can be lost (like throwing away the ship's rudder). Because the last half of a design process becomes so intense, there is a tendency to set aside the Vision and its role as a guiding force. It is important to find a way to keep the Vision on the table. We always tried to name a "Keeper of the Vision." If that person can make sure the Vision is not put in a closet, there is a better chance all things in the final plan will be put in the proper context.

Finally, a Vision should not be confused with a plan, a concept, or a Master Plan. Those come later as more specific products. If a Vision is stated too specifically, and near-term initiatives don't turn out quite that way, it can be perceived as out of date and quickly placed in the "obsolete" file. Unfortunately, *an out-of-sight Vision is an out-of-mind Vision.*

Skeptics tend to refer to the visioning process as a product of elusive daydreaming or "blue-sky" irrelevance. That can certainly be true, but such a Vision usually fades away. With care, a Vision statement can combine relevance and practical achievability with the inspiration of a "big idea."

In Fig. 28, the horizontal arrows illustrate the idea of a continuing presence of the Vision throughout the process. It only needs occasional attention and sharpening along the way, allowing direct effects on projects. It might be said that a Vision is so basic there should be little call for revisions. But certain adjustments are called for, and the Vision might adjust to accommodate changing circumstances or unforeseen events.

When leaders join in carrying the Vision forward, it has the best chance to endure. Leaders, both public and private, need to know the Vision well, help frame it, believe in it, and be able to reference it with ease when relevant.

The Barnsdall Art Park in Los Angeles is another example of an enduring Vision based on a long-term preservation strategy. At the heart of the city near the corner of Sunset and Hollywood Boulevards, a single and distinctive hill stands alone surrounded by intense urban development. Olive groves cover the hillsides, and the quiet hilltop is graced by an

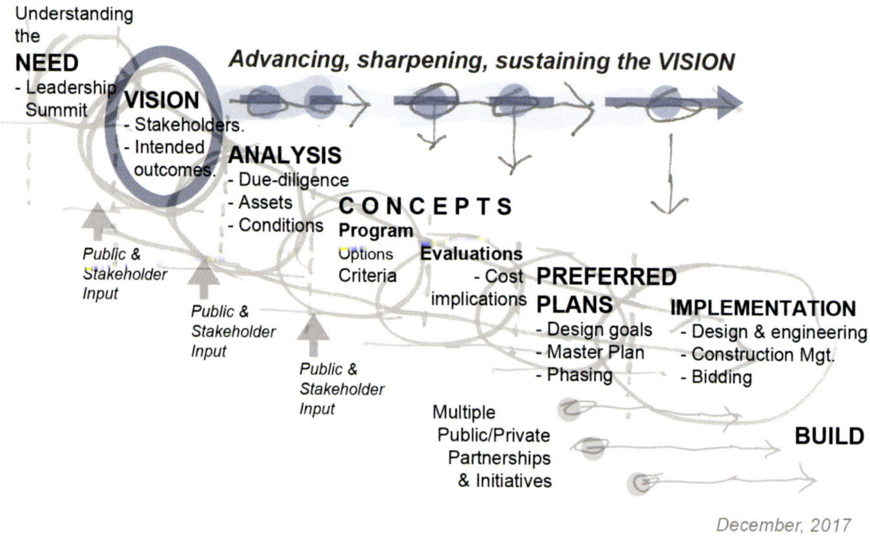

FIG. 28: A continuing presence of the Vision throughout the process.

exquisite residence designed by Frank Lloyd Wright. It was here that the Barnsdall family established this iconic home with its classic art, sculpture, and gardens in the 1920s. Much of the hill was soon gifted to the City of Los Angeles as Barnsdall Park for public enjoyment of the arts, and it became a landmark in central LA for more than 70 years. In the 1990s, a desire to broaden Barnsdall Park into a distinctive cultural center led to Peter Walker William Johnson and Partners (PWWJ)'s involvement to determine the new program and related plan. Approaching the site with a Framework mindset and a deliberate, broadly based public involvement process, the following Vision was cast and embedded in its mission:

> *The mission of the Barnsdall Art Park Foundation is to ensure that Barnsdall Art Park is a vibrant, inclusive space for creativity, cultural expression, civic conversation, and social empowerment.*

More than 25 years later, the inspirational strategy based on historic recall continues to unfold. The Barnsdall restoration was one of a kind! And what a privilege it was to be part of the team. Sustaining the Vision is

FIG. 29: Context of Barnsdall Park with the olive grove, c.1947 (credits: Stephen & Christy McAvoy Family Trust, Los Angeles Public Library).

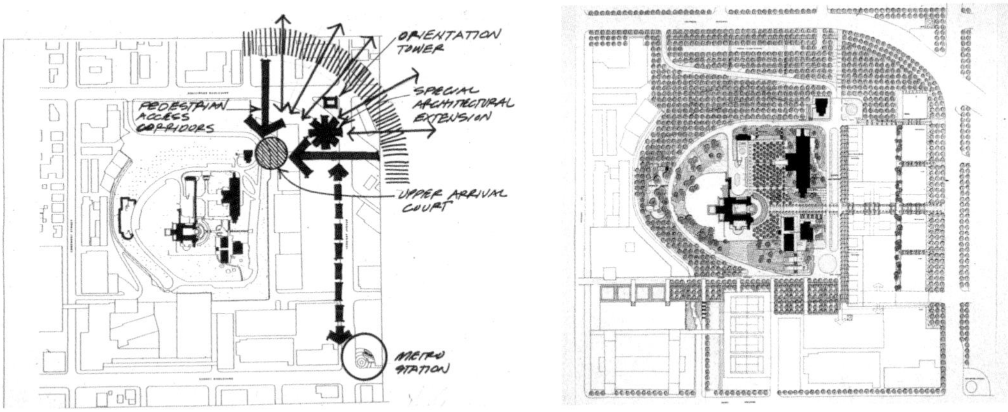

FIG. 30: Framework diagram and master plan showing the visual and circulation extensions in relation to the olive grove and the urban context (master plan credits: PWP Landscape Architecture).

a worthy endeavor. The highlight for me remains vivid ... the enthusiasm of the local stakeholders. Our work session participants were open to ideas and energetic about them. It is this kind of stakeholder excitement, in my mind, that sustains a vibrant history like the Barnsdall story—one that can honor the past while shaping the future! What a bargain!

In summary, to be effective, Vision statements and related diagrams need to be brief, articulate, and memorable—adaptable to easy and frequent reference. This calls for a high degree of stakeholder input and leadership commitment to the long view. Well-conceived Visions of this kind, commonly held by most, can become critically important and enduring roadmaps for the future.

CHAPTER FOUR

DISCOVERY

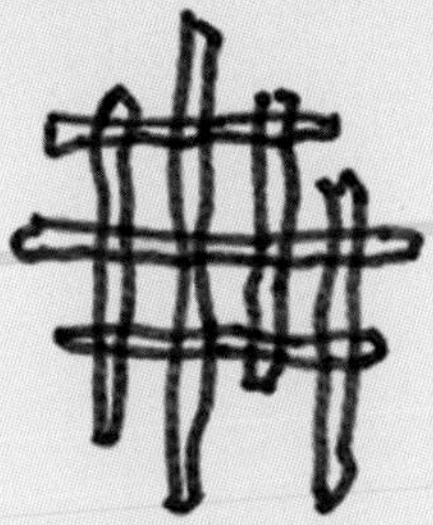

THE BONES

Exploring and Resolving a Preferred, Long-Term Direction

As the name implies, this "Bones" icon emphasizes the few, strong strokes of an emerging plan. As a graphic portrayal it begins to look like a plan but is intentionally short on detail. Every worthy Concept plan has a set of Bones, or what are often called "key moves." Isolating the primary moves of a planning concept helps discussions to effectively get at the essence of an emergent plan.

THE BONES

In the design process, a sequence of emerging planning ideas shifts from broad to narrow: from a Vision to a framework plan, on to concept plans, followed by a master plan, culminating with a series of detailed design/build decisions. The planning/design term Bones comes to the forefront midway in the design process by summing up the context-centered insights gained by working groups.

When the many options considered thus far can be summarized into a portrayal of a long-term direction, it is important to pause. This point in the process occurs at a time prior to a focus on concept plans, and an intentional pause allows a chance to affirm unity of thinking. This is the opportune moment to check team signals, because there is about to be a shift in team members from those with a long-term Vision and those with the shorter-term interest of getting the Vision built. They represent two very different mindsets calling for special attention to communicating well.

A graphic portrayal needs to occur as early as possible to gain traction on the framework direction(s) before conceptual plans are put forth.

Portrayal

There is no set of rules guiding what a Bones diagram should look like, but there are some basic expectations. It should feature a relatively simple set of points of the highest priority with strong graphic expression.

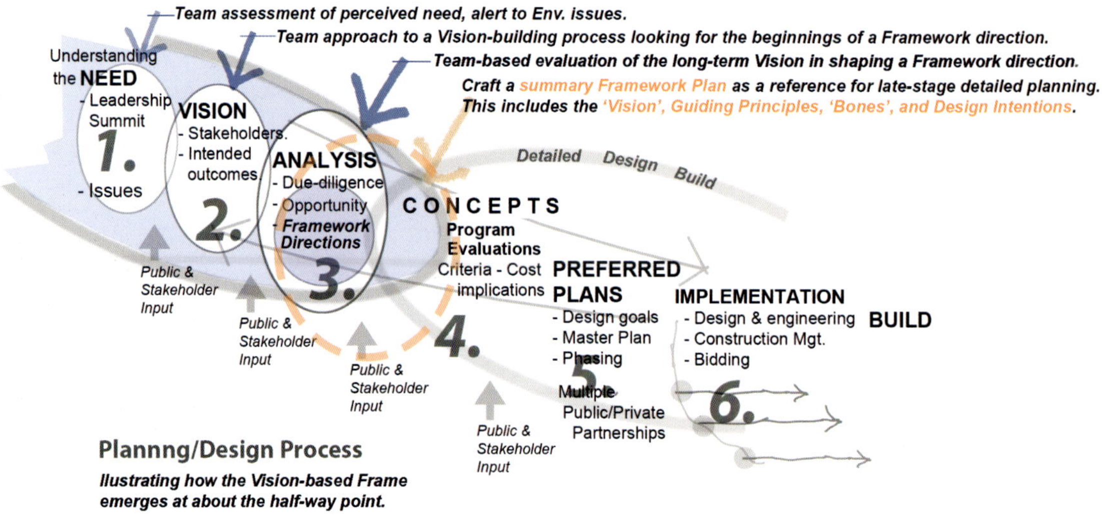

It expresses the Vision but goes further to recognize physical conditions and implies a physical plan but carefully avoids looking like one. It is largely a matter of iterative testing—building confidence that all things are beginning to fit. This is all in preparation for the detailed concept plans to follow.

FIG. 31: The shift from broad to narrow in the emerging ideas during a planning/design process and how the Vision-based frame or Bones emerges at a key, overlapping halfway point.

Process Hazard

It is at this point that those managing the process can move on into the conceptual drawing stage without carrying the long-term *Framework Direction* with them. When this is the case, there is a potential for not putting the right things in the right places ... a simple case of losing perspective. One of the reasons for this book is to increase the chances that this will not happen.

There was a JJR penchant for always seeking the larger context. It was, in part, a reflection of the designer's basic inclinations, but also probably came from an acquired awareness that any given part is understood best when considered in its context. In design discussions at the Harvard GSD, Professor Hideo Sasaki often called it the "structure of a plan." In his critique sessions, his first questions were all about understanding the plan's structure. He would explain how knowing the basic structure of a proposed plan enabled him to critique the rest of the plan much more effectively. My classmate Peter Walker's term was "the basic Idea." Later, some have referred to it as *the Vision* or *the Frame*.

In any case, *each term implies a very important view of the whole—the basic physical direction of an imagined future*.

Any community development involves two fundamental parts. The first is the lineal system patterns supporting development (utilities, transportations, pedestrian/bikeways, and greenways). The second is fixed object patterns (building footprints, parking, and automobile circulation patterns). We learned early on that development guidelines based on the support systems are much more enduring over time than building locations and form. The diagram-like format helps to reinforce a planning direction without specific reference to design form.

Examples of Framework Diagrams Featuring the Bones

The examples below of Framework diagrams are summaries of the most basic direction each plan took. Selected from various project types, these diagrams demonstrate the structure of the place discovered through the planning and design process. They also show how there can be many ways of illustrating the Framework, featuring a simple set of points based on the highest priority through strong graphic expression.

These examples are not yet measured plans; those come in the next phase—the detailed conceptual plan options. But they show the solutions to hoped-for Visions.

The University of Washington Campus Expansion

Bothell, WA | 1998–2002
Collaborators: NBBJ

FIG. 32: Framework diagram for the University of Washington-Cascadia Community College campus expansion developed after two years of exploration, and a momentous morning of discovery which led to this lineal campus concept.

To accommodate continuing growth needs, the University initiated plans in 1997 to build an expansion campus in a new location. The State of Washington mandated that such a branch campus must include a new location for Cascadia Community College as well. The chosen site was just south of the community of Bothell, at the confluence of two state freeways, I-405 and I-522. The site featured an upper shelf and a lower shelf divided by a 40-foot change of grade. It was a groundwater seepage bank and sensitive to nearby construction disturbance.

The upland shelf featured a remnant conifer grove which could stabilize construction impact and provide an important neighborhood buffer. The lowland shelf was at one time a wetland with a meandering stream, but a circa 1900 log chute dried up the site to buildable soil conditions.

After more than two years of attempts to stitch together a campus plan suitable for a major university and a community college, the development strategy illustrated in this simple diagram received applause from both ends. The slope between an existing upper forested buffer and a lower stream restoration suggested a lineal campus with an entry identity at each end, the larger for the University of Washington, the smaller for Cascadia Community College. A central library is located equidistant between them. The idea included building a groundwater treatment plant and returning the original stream flow and its wetland condition to the lower shelf. In a few strong strokes, the design frame reveals the long-term development strategy. All other elements of the campus quickly fell into place. Both the University and the College called it a substantial victory.

(NOTE: See Pages 105 to 110 for a case study on the project and the types of spatial language used in the early discovery phase.)

The Downtown Waterfront Vision

Holland, MI | 2020–present

Collaborators: GMB, Hitchcock Design Group, Har Ye Kan, Nick Rolinski, Boileau & Co.

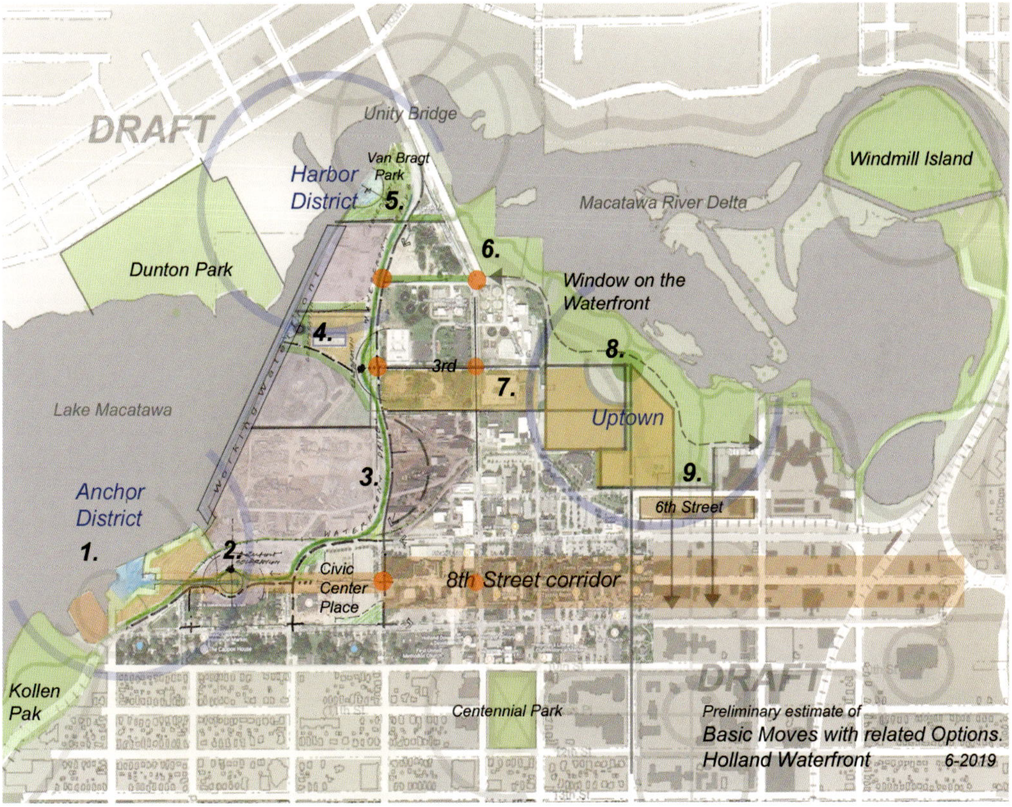

FIG. 33: Framework diagram for the Downtown Waterfront Vision for Holland, MI highlighting the key opportunities for connectivity, redevelopment, and the strengthening the Community's waterfront.

This example from the Downtown Holland story shows how a chosen location is increasingly detailed from Vision to Frame, then Concept to Plan, while holding to the broadly stated Vision.

The former coal-fired municipal power plant operated by the Holland Board of Public Works was set to be decommissioned in the 2010s, which offered an opportunity to explore a publicly owned waterfront property prominently located on Lake Macatawa. It triggered the call for a holistic look at waterfront development beyond this site that would build on the City's Downtown Vision.

Through a series of community workshops and several design workshops, the Framework yielded three potential redevelopment districts, all connected by a long green line integrated with the Macatawa Greenway system. It represents a continuous "on the waterfront" theme for pedestrians and cyclists, weaving through a major community park on the southwest, a gateway green at the bridge crossing, and then into the naturalistic setting of Window on the Waterfront park on the east.

An *unbroken continuity* for this greenway system is the key ingredient for downtown Holland's long-term waterfront development strategy. That is the "Backbone." This annotated diagram is a different format for summarizing the Bones while at the same time describing a Framework direction.

The University of Michigan Central Campus Plan

Ann Arbor, MI | 1963–present
Collaborators: Johnson, Johnson & Roy, Inc. (JJR)

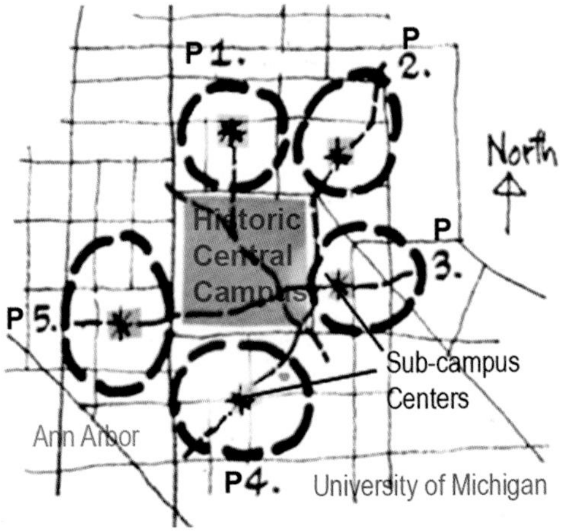

FIG. 34: Framework diagram for the University of Michigan's Central Campus showing the future areas for growth, each with its distinctive identity yet connected to the historic Central Campus via diagonal walking patterns first formed by cow paths in the former pasture.

The assignment to prepare a series of long-range development plans for the University of Michigan's Central Campus began in 1961 and prevailed for the better part of 25 years. This work early in my career introduced a fresh approach to campus planning and development at a time when the demand for such was on a dramatic rise. It became a model for strategic physical planning through the 1960s and 1970s.

A decade before the Civil War, a 40-acre farm in the middle of the sleepy town of Ann Arbor was the setting for the early campus. Several academic buildings of brick and granite were built along the street edges. The emerging campus was fenced to contain the grazing of cows even as the student paths began to form. The cow paths blended with student/faculty walkways, forming the diagonal walking patterns so iconic in today's campus, like "The Diag."

This Campus expansion diagram is a study in simplicity, showing growth areas in five academic precincts, each with a distinctive central identity. Five primary academic corridors move from the campus center through the center of each precinct, and on to a parking supply. Scale is confirmed by the shaded 40-acre square—the historic central campus where the farm stood—and the existing streets. Such basic insights were easily aligned with the University of Michigan's policymaking.

The plan was simple. Anyone could draw it. This basic growth strategy endured for the next 25 years and is still a factor setting directions for continued campus infill. It illustrates a long-term growth Vision with hints of design characteristics along the way.

Stanford University,

Palo Alto, CA | c. 1990s–2000s
Collaborators: David J. Neuman, FAIA, PWWJ

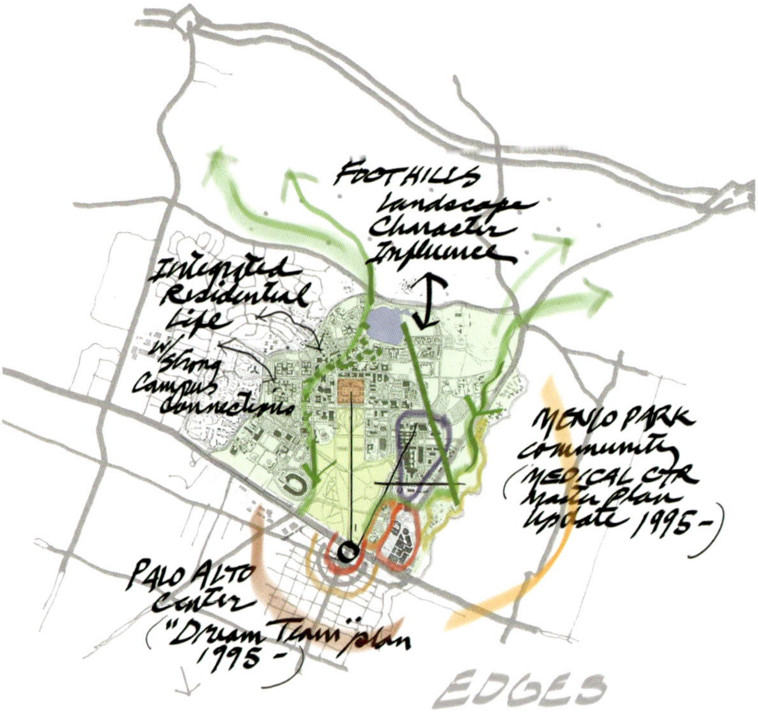

FIG. 33. Character edges of the Stanford University campus, with the "river of live oaks descending from the foothills to the bay".

Planning assignments with Stanford University began in the early 1990s out of the Peter Walker William Johnson and Partners (PWWJ) office in collaboration with Stanford University architect, David J. Neuman, FAIA. A primary focus was reestablishing the power of Frederick Law Olmsted's original 1888 master plan. Known as the "Plan of Central Premises," Olmsted sought to establish Palm Drive as the central axis, with sight lines running parallel and perpendicular to this axis offering views through the campus. After the rapid postwar campus expansion that saw the proliferation of parking lots and cluttering of buildings within the campus core, a new effort led by Neuman was energized to restore the clarity of Olmsted's plan.

In analyzing the foundational direction and the contextual character of the campus, a new Framework Plan was developed. It brought back Olmsted's idea of an east-west Serra Mall (now the Jane Stanford Way) axis reinforced by a series of quadrangles and set out to connect the foothills to the bay. The reinvigorated Framework Plan also called for a distinctive, tree-lined Campus Drive Loop to unify the campus and define an "academic growth boundary".

In parallel with the Framework Plan, a new notion emerged whereby the Medical Center might relate directly to the campus by expanding the School of Medicine along Serra Mall. This was a key transformation where, for the first time,

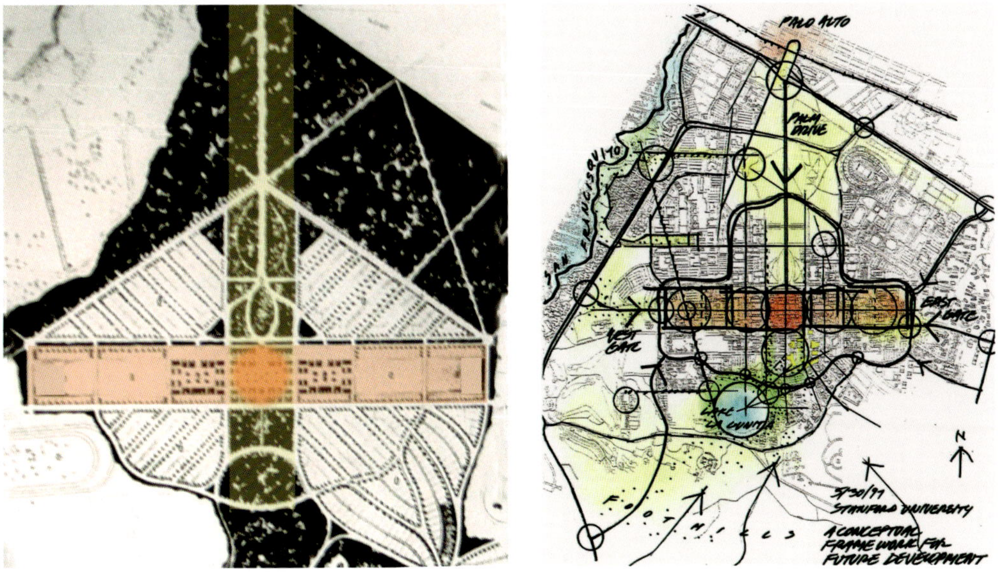

the back door of the existing Medical Center can become a front door on Serra Mall. Primary vehicular traffic was to be kept west along Welch and Oak Road, while Serra Mall became the major, campus-wide transit/bike/pedestrian corridor.

Together, these important design intentions enabled Stanford University to embrace its past and develop an enduring Framework to support its ongoing and future expansion.

FIG. 36: Key design elements highlighted in the 1888 "Plan of Central Premises" by Olmsted and their re-establishment in the 1999 Framework Plan.

Trinity Christian College

Palos Heights, IL | 2018–present
Collaborators: GMB

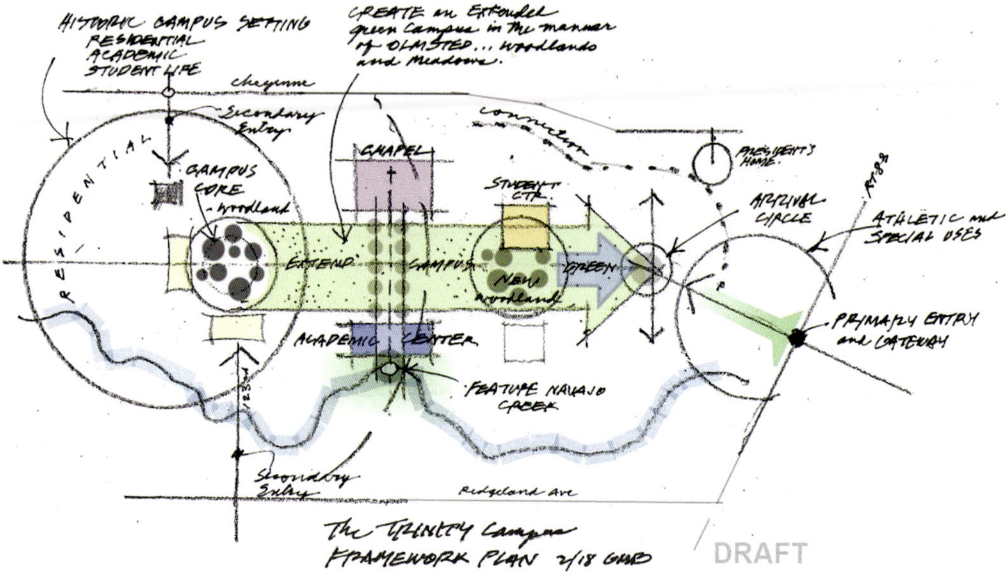

A small, private liberal arts college in the Chicago metropolitan area, Trinity Christian College sought to develop a "21st-century campus master plan that solidifies Trinity's campus as an acknowledged place of vibrancy, beauty, and significance."

Five guiding principles were developed collaboratively by the Campus Master Plan Steering Committee and GMB. These principles included: (i) Envision a holistic campus, (ii) Celebrate the Kingdom, (iii) Foster community, (iv) Address boundaries, and (v) Reveal identity landmarks. They are intended to guide the development of the planning process and long-term Framework thinking.

To support future growth and expansion, the proposed framework and master plan enhances the north-south orientation of the campus, running in parallel to the natural meandering edge of the Navajo Creek to the east. This modest, meandering stream became the most surprising form-giving idea for the campus Framework. Instead of treating it as a drainage basin, the Vision and master plan made it a distinctive, meaningful new campus feature, woven into the new academic building as a celebration of the beauty of the place.

In stretching the campus, three core campus facilities are proposed to be removed and replaced

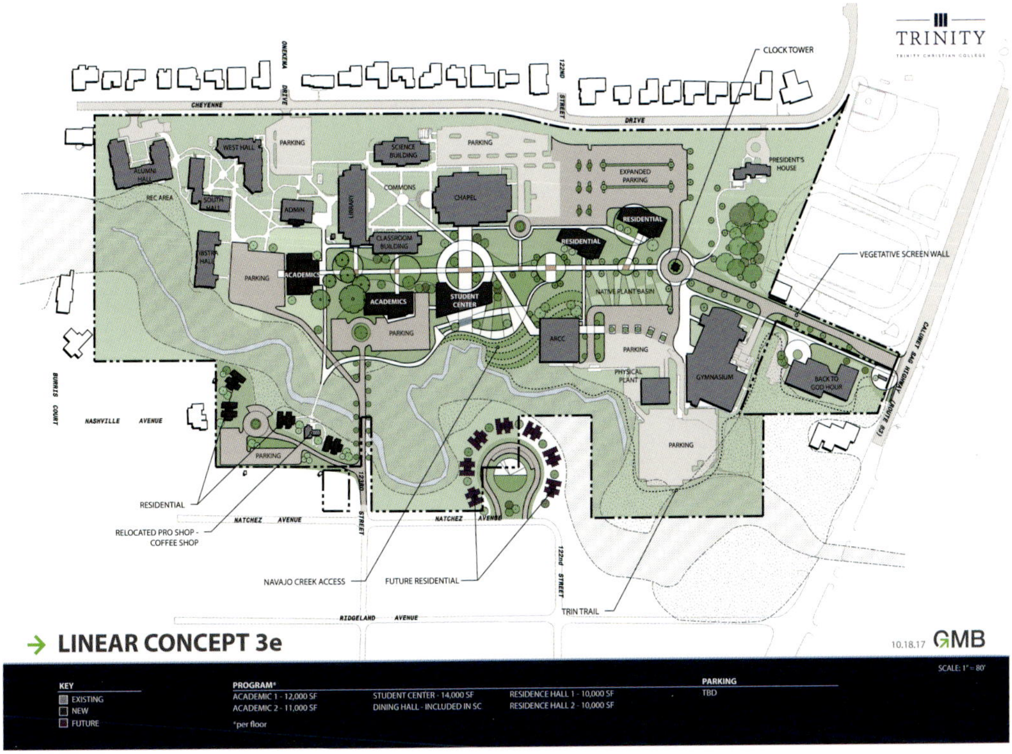

FIG. 37: Framework plan for Trinity Christian College, showing the prevailing influence of the Navajo Creek and the historic cluster of oak and maple trees as key form drivers. This early discovery and framework synthesis set the stage for more detailed design in the master plan (credits: William Johnson & GMB).

with new structures: the academic building, a student center, and several new residential buildings. A new campus woodland to the north serves as a counterpoint to the historic cluster of oaks and maples. Together with a gateway roundabout from the West College Drive entrance, they reinforce this north-south orientation and complete a new campus cluster to the north. To the south, two new residential clusters flank the eastern entrance from 123rd Street, stitching the campus with the surrounding neighborhood.

SPATIAL LANGUAGE

Utilizing the Power of Hand-Drawn Graphics

Consider this "Spatial Language" icon depicting hand-eye coordination. Those of us with the gift of sight see our world with multi-dimensional wonder. Sharing what we see takes a special language of the hand, eye, heart, and mind to convey spatial information along with an emotion. It is called "Drawing," but with a special purpose in mind.

SPATIAL LANGUAGE

JJR's signature mark of distinction was the expressive hand-drawn quick sketch and diagram. But it wasn't the first.

Hand-drawn images are as old as the first attempt at human discourse. Think of the stone against stone drawings of early cave people, the intriguing wall drawings found in the ruins of Pompei, and then the richness of every kind of painting throughout the history of civilization. Hand-based drawing is too embedded in the human soul to think it might be displaced by technological innovation.

But there is much promise in the seamless blending of the two. The spoken and written words are each a language of their own. In the same way, the drawn image is a distinctive visual language unto itself. Like any language, there are variations; the "Spatial Language" we refer to here is from the visual language assortment. Familiar to design professionals in the exchange of ideas about form and spatial relationships, 2D and 3D sketches are of a distinctive spatial language, now highly computer-based and much revered by urban planning/design firms.

It was true with JJR as well, but in those early days there was a difference. We made clear and compelling diagrams and sketches that told important, solution-oriented stories. They happened early in the process, and many were created while the client group watched. Rough as they often were, they were central to the summary findings, not just supplemental. It looked easy (but was not) and intriguing. The casual sense of excellence they represented went a long way in building trust.

Sketching freehand quickly and in simple terms are the essentials for seeing more than meets the eye. The keys are to introduce these early; to undertake the sketches by hand using pencil, chalk, or marker; to be spontaneous and inviting; and to focus on issues for problem solving. *These drawings are not intended to be precious, admired, or celebrated. The value is in that which is discovered and caused along the way. The process of drawing and the drawings themselves are tools and a means, not an end.*

For young people aspiring to be in one of the physical planning/design professions, certain questions arise about hand drawing (that is, drawing directly with the hand, not with computer sketching program). The most basic question: *is it necessary?*

On the one hand the answer is an emphatic *"yes,"* since, in my view, it is the gateway to seeing the world more clearly. On the other hand, for many the answer is a practical *"no,"* since computer graphics are increasingly improving and can produce pencil-like drawings—even the very rough diagrammatic graphics that we praise so readily. The problem is that it still takes skillful input to achieve the computer's beautiful output.

If the answer is "Yes, I want to learn to draw," the next question is *"Can I draw?"*

Most anyone can draw far beyond their expectations. I know this from my years of teaching sketching to landscape architecture grad students at the University of Michigan. To their surprise, most learned quickly to make informative pencil/pen drawings. The techniques were simple and very basic. They could refine the process later, using techniques of their choice.

The most compelling answer to the question "Why draw at all?" is this: *"I draw so that others might see their ideas more clearly"* (their ideas, not mine). That's my answer. In shaping the places we live, the purpose of drawing is also to increase hand–eye–heart–mind coordination, enhance place awareness, foster spontaneity in the search for ideas, influence early design directions, and assist others to see more while inducing creative dialogue.

The way hand-based sketching is used at an early stage of the design process can work wonders in group dynamics. It can bring others comfortably into the dialogue while quickly informing them of ideas they never knew they had. It is a way of opening the mind. Drawing by hand with stakeholders disarms their inclinations to challenge and increases their readiness to learn. Lessons learned can be directly transferred to improving one's ability to work more effectively with computer graphics.

The tactile "see it now" immediacy of hand-drawn sketches done on the spot during work sessions is priceless in the idea-building process. Stakeholders and public participants grow to trust the simplicity of the language. In that trust, their fear of preconceptions diminishes, and they tend to join in more freely with shaping ideas. People have more ideas in them than they realize. This simple sketching language can help bring out the ideas from hiding.

At one of our interviews for a prospective project of major scale, we were asked to conduct a four-hour work session presided over by the client. He was known to be a skeptical CEO. Our team strategy was simple: Get Dr. Black to draw! Four hours flew by and before we knew it, Dr. Black couldn't help it and was drawing away. He loved the process, and the rest is history.

FIG. 38: Drawing: Seeing through the curtain of doubt to say, "I can do this!".

As this anecdote suggests, anyone can draw. There are only a couple of key obstacles. The first is not so much the challenge of learning to draw; rather, it is the quick assumption "I can't draw" or "I don't see a compelling purpose." I believe most people can draw in the manner discussed here, with both power and purpose, *if* one so chooses. The key is to move through a certain curtain of doubt to be able to say, "I can do this" or "It really does make a difference."

Drawing: A Partnership Between Hand-Based & Digital Graphics

As JJR grew larger and refined its planning and design practice, the focus on building early dialogue with client groups continued and our casual signature graphics played an important role, even though computer graphics were rapidly advancing. At JJR some colleagues developed great

FIG. 39: Drawing: A partnership between hand-based and digital graphics.

skill with early sketching and informative diagrams, like James Turner, Don Hildebrandt, Jim Richards, and Stan Doctor. When they went to other places they carried with them the hand-drawing mindset.

During the early exploration of the problem-solving design process, the drawings were loose, nimble, and spontaneous. By drawing early, freely, quickly, and often, effective sketches and diagrams can be generated, thereby influencing early design directions. More importantly, drawing makes the early process visible to all who are contributing. Toward the later part of the design process, the drawings get more complicated, refined, and precise as ideas are resolved and finalized.

There is an important kind of learning uniquely gained from a hand-based drawing skill. When it is blended with computer graphics, a kind of partnership occurs, increasing the productivity of both. Accordingly, a freshly conceived "learning module" approach to the teaching of hand drawing throughout one's design education would go a long way in advancing a natural partnership. This kind of drawing is about two things:

(i) Layers: multiple layers enable ways of seeing, relating, and ordering.
(ii) Tonal values have priority over lines.

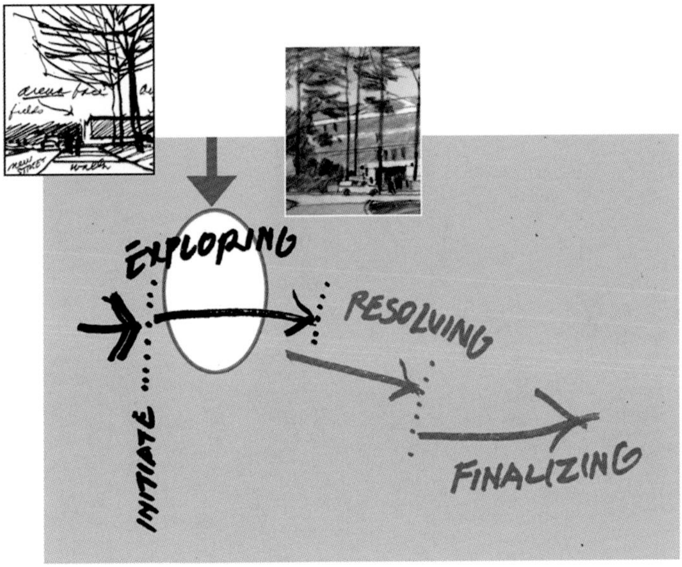

FIG. 40: Drawing: The use of layers and tones in the discovery process.

Our world has many layers and tonal qualities, and our sketches follow suit in layers and tones. While our instinct may be to hold the pencil or pen tightly and to draw with lines, in the layers and tones mindset the pencil is held loosely to shape tonal variations. In the case of a pen, tones can be built with varied line densities.

By working small as a start, on 3" × 5" cards, a discipline is fostered in the drawings to focus on the overview and the tonal values. Each layer is finished before moving forward, with sharper baselines defining layers. At the same time, the drawings would be informed by:

- CONTRASTS: dark to light distinctions.
- COMPOSITION: creates interest and intrigue.
- WHITES: know where whites go.
- GRAYS: understand first, then color.
- QUICKNESS: produces freshness.
- PURPOSE: each drawing with a message.

Those at JJR worked hard on developing a visual language. We felt that important messages should be short and clear. Creating the right

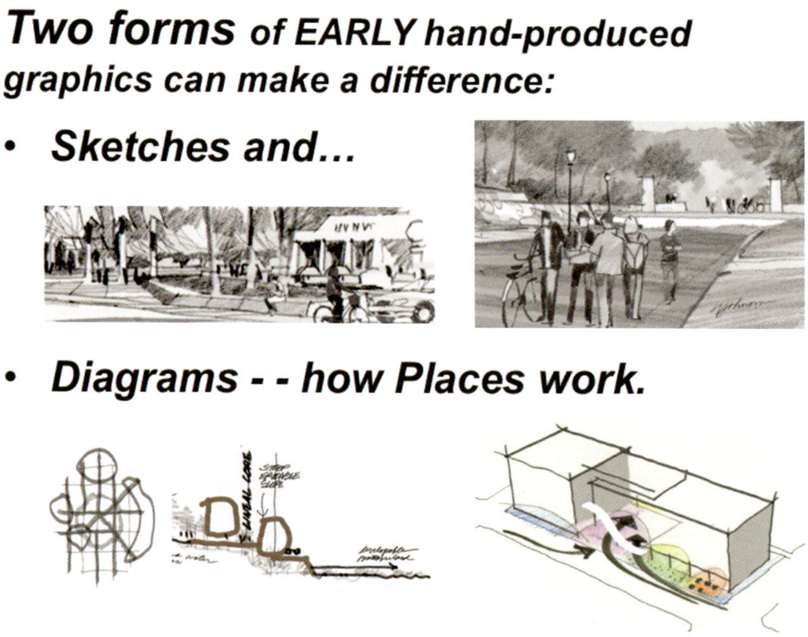

FIG. 41: Drawing: A partnership between hand-based and digital graphics with 1) sketches showing how places might look and feel, 2) diagrams showing how places might work.

diagrarn, at the right time, became a very special kind of art. In particular, two forms of early hand-produced drawings can make a difference: sketches and diagrams.

Broadly speaking, there are seven types of spatial language drawings:

- Spontaneous, Free-form: for noting observations, information, and ideas.
- Photo/Model Tracings: framed as perspectives to refine the sketch content.
- Drawings with Notational Emphasis: to increase awareness and understanding.
- Diagramming in Free-Form: to explore Visions, ideas, and concepts.
- Diagramming to Scale: over aerials, photos, and models to express the Bones.
- Sectional Drawings: to increase design clarity and detail, sometimes with a one-point perspective.
- Refined Visual Stories: selected combinations of drawings to refine the "stories" and keep the drawings loose and fresh.

FIG. 42: Spontaneous, free-form drawings with notational emphasis showing the context and initial options for the University of Washington-Cascadia Community College Campus.

Project Sample: The University of Washington-Cascadia Community College

The following project sample expands on the University of Washington-Cascadia Community College in Bothell, Washington, described earlier in the Bones. It demonstrates the use of these seven different spatial language drawings at different points in a problem-solving process.

In 1995, the State of Washington initiated steps for the creation of a new commuter campus and mandating it would be the joint location of Cascadia Community College and a branch of the University of Washington.

Enrollments were to be consistent with other campus extensions in the region of a similar character and were to be fitting for the site circumstances.

The site chosen for the two campuses was at the intersection of I-405 and I-522, just west of Downtown Bothell. In the 1880s, the site had been part of the Truly Farm, marked by cottages and a hillside residence within an active logging community. By the 1990s, the upper shelf was a remnant conifer forest and was separated from the farm and nursery in the lower shelf by steep slopes and a historic log flume.

The initial concepts worked around the sensitive slope conditions and the Truly Farmstead, focusing the potential campus developments in the upland and lowland areas. In these options, 15 acres of slope were preserved; by contrast, the potential development meant the loss of the 35-acre remnant conifer forest. One option would also impact the historic log flume and the 85-acre lower shelf.

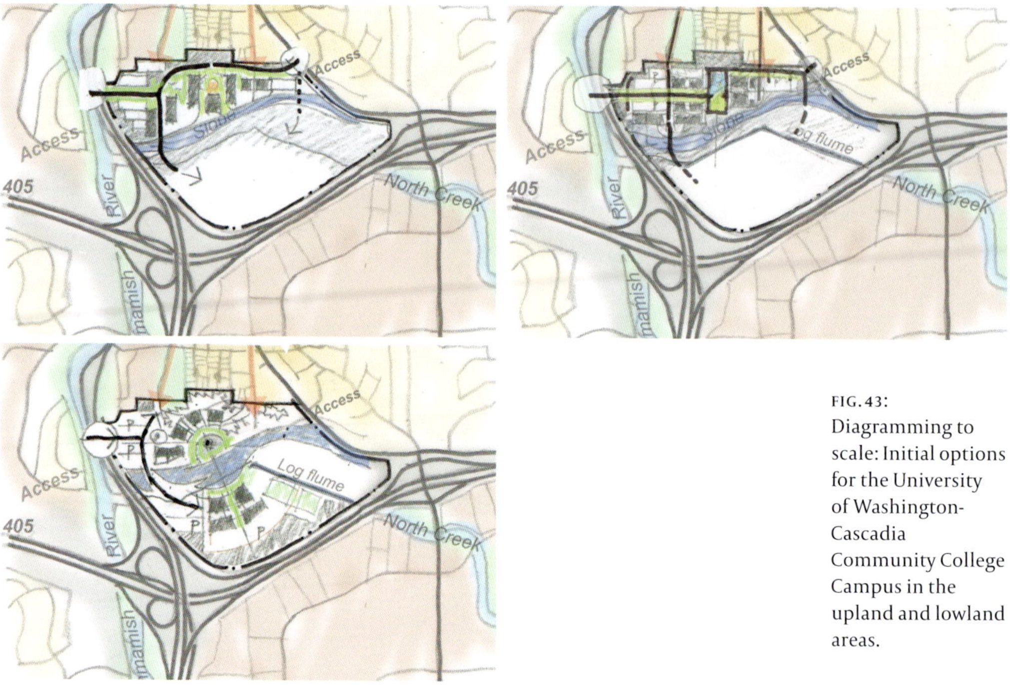

FIG. 43: Diagramming to scale: Initial options for the University of Washington-Cascadia Community College Campus in the upland and lowland areas.

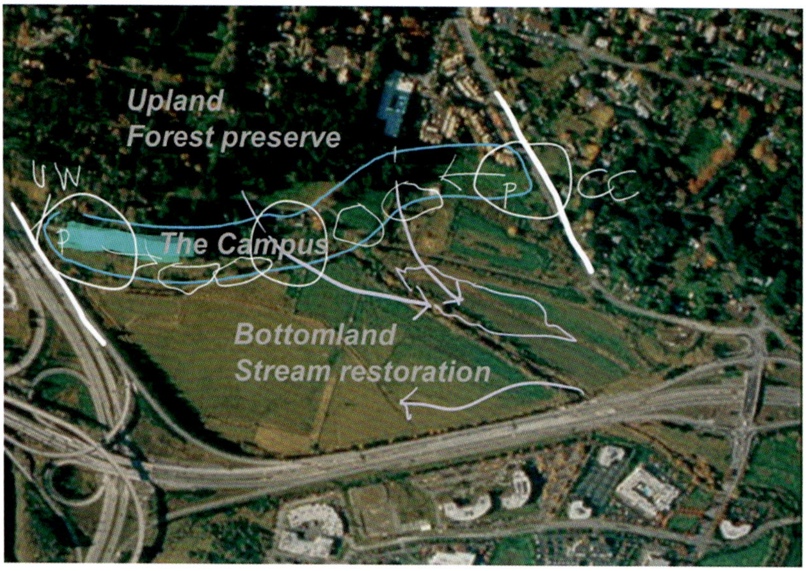

FIG. 44: Free-form drawing with notational emphasis showing the eventual direction for a lineal campus.

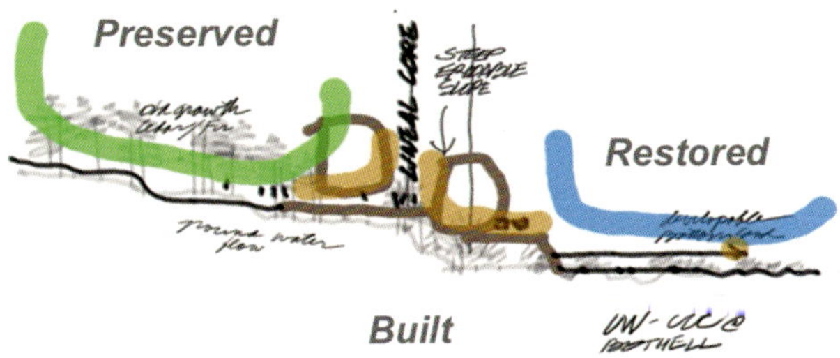

FIG. 45: Loose section drawing showing the lineal campus in relation to the topography and preservation/restoration intentions.

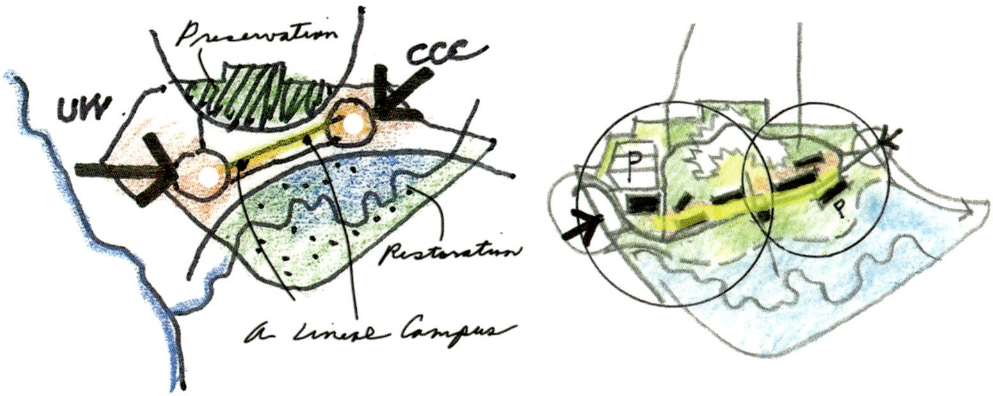

FIG. 46: Two diagrams to scale showing the eventual idea to create a connected, lineal campus on the slopes, preserve the upper conifer forest, and to restore the stream to its native condition. Loose building forms and parking areas are shown as possible areas for development.

Both the University of Washington and Cascadia Community College, however, felt that there could be better outcomes. Returning to the drawing board, the design team took an inside-out approach by exploring the steep slope as a connector between the two access points. Working with the contours of the slope, the notion of a "lineal campus" was born, with separate gateways for each institution but a shared academic commons. The revised concept preserved the upland forest while restoring the lowland stream to its native condition. What a win!

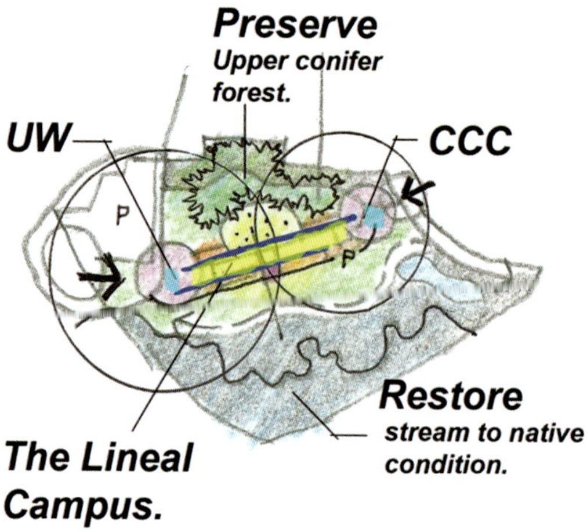

FIG. 47: A further articulated Framework plan highlighting key elements and intentions.

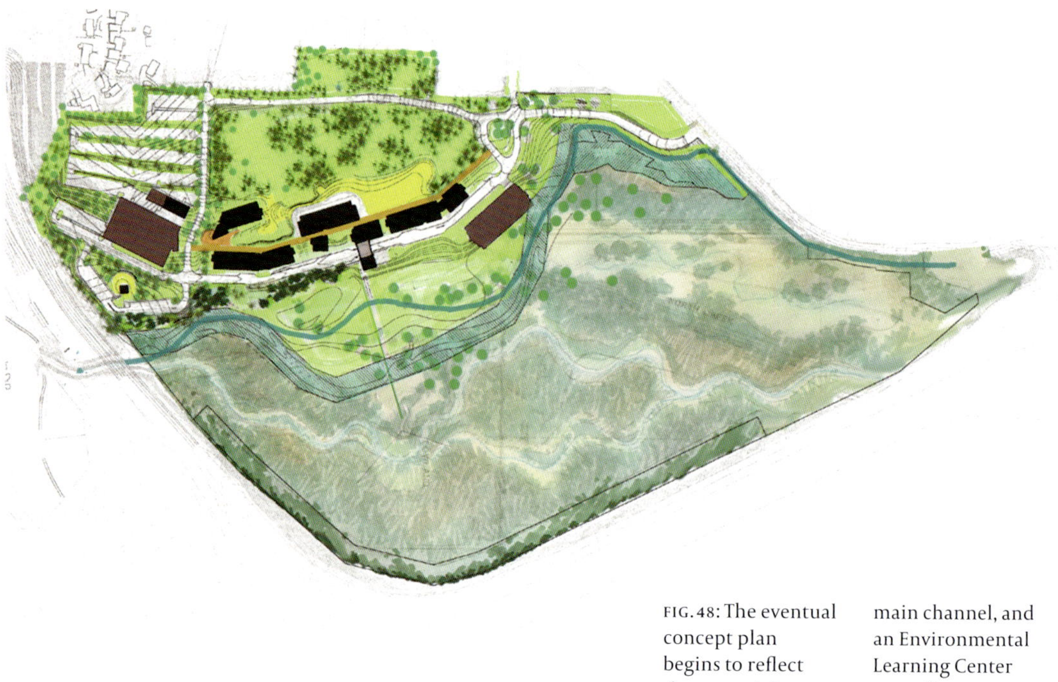

FIG. 48: The eventual concept plan begins to reflect the potential building footprints, the restored meandering path of the North Creek main channel, and an Environmental Learning Center extending perpendicular to the lineal campus at the midway point (credits: NBBJ).

FIG. 49: Photographs showing the developed campus along the lineal connector and the soft landscape transition towards the native stream restoration on the lowland area (credits: © Timothy Griffith).

Knowing when to draw for and with the client and community is just as important as knowing how to draw and what to draw. In any given process, there are dedicated drawing periods as in a typical design workshop/charrette process. There are also brief, spontaneous windows when a quick sketch can be especially helpful for the participants. These are flashing moments that can go by fast early in the game when the instinct to draw may not be as obvious. The onus is thus on the planning/design professionals as facilitators to pay special attention and to make the most of what a quick, back-of-the-envelope sketch can achieve. They are especially constructive at certain times:

- When key ideas, input, and observations emerge about a place and its people.
- When design premises are tested.
- When seeking clarification or making a point.
- When inviting others to draw without fear of judgment.
- When summing up to achieve consensus and understanding.

Today, the use of hand-drawn graphics—pencil, in particular—is very limited. The tools of choice are computer based and there is an unfortunate loss of spontaneity in the creative process. Despite the important lessons that can be learned via the pencil, it is likely that other computer-based drawing tools can reveal the same lessons and are highly pertinent in the digital working environment today. The key is to move through a curtain of doubt to be able to say, "I can do this!" or "It really does make a difference!"

CHAPTER FIVE

RESOLUTION

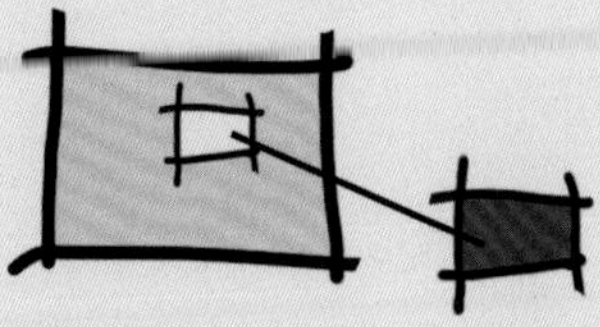

DESIGN AS FORM

Shaping Places of Design Distinction Consistent with the Vision

This "Design as Form" icon emphasizes a concentrated focus on physical form (the small dark square) driven by a direct relationship to its context (the larger square representing community). Context is the natural and cultural world in which the focus area fits. The potential benefits flow in both directions. There is a ready source of Design Form inspiration inherent in the community circumstances at hand. In return, innovative Design Form based on context insights can help celebrate that community bringing about an awareness of place at a level not otherwise found . . . free of charge. That's quite a bargain!

DESIGN AS FORM

Whatever aspect of the community is under study, some of the greatest pleasures are discovering early stage clues to physical form and watching the steady emergence of final form. It is at this point that creative problem-solving crystallizes into the art of natural and built environments. What emerges is a deliberate and purposeful outcome utilizing design principles that can be flexibly applied to development initiatives at any scale. The power of a skillfully achieved art form cannot be overemphasized.

Problem-solving and art share a creative source, but they show up in different ways in different people because of varied talents and skills. Some may find themselves more in the arena of problem solving; others tend toward art form. The former tends to be process-driven while the latter is associated with spontaneous revelations. At the same time, both are part of a single continuum because creative problem-solving is a legitimate search for art. There is an art *of* and art *within* problem-solving; conversely, there is a problem-solving *within* and *behind* the art.

A Context-Centered Mindset

By the time JJR was formed in 1963, Carl, Clarence, and I had our own notions about the way one works to design enduring places for people. It was clear from our many discussions to determine a consistent office approach that we shared a context-centered mindset to iterative design processes. *It was this context-centered mindset that encouraged creative design considerations at the earliest stages of work.* It brought continuity into and throughout the several phases. We knew that ideas about the final form can pop up at any time, not limited by the lineal format of the typical design process. It was meant to be deliberate yet loose.

We also shared firm clarity in knowing the way we practice—we knew our identities and "lanes" in the Playing Field of broader community building professions. Yet we also had a proclivity to move beyond these lanes. Landscape architecture is not confined to coming in at the tail end of a process to add the final touches; it can intentionally provide the big picture, contextual insights, in the early stages of ideation and strategic decision making. Working in multidisciplinary teams, we identified patterns in the connected systems within the built, natural, and cultural realms, making the professional edges the center of integrative thinking.

The icon for "Design as Form" emphasizes the continuity of the overall context starting with finding form, then giving form to community as a whole, before shaping smaller-scale form detail within a community. The overall icon represents a legible, unified future of possibilities. In any given form, the context quietly persists, such that it is not possible to talk about or understand any single piece without the whole. *Hence, the emergent "art" and "design as form" are about both the "community form" and the "object form."* This could be a road that inspires at a bend by framing a view or unfolding into a new one. It could also be the layout of buildings that shape green spaces; conversely, it could be the broader landscape and landforms that mold the architectural response to a site.

A holistic approach to design form is increasingly the primary objective in the design world. The intentional process of context-centered understandings, discoveries, and Vision-building continue to provide a relevant set of physical development guidelines in crafting distinctive landscape and urban design form. Transformational ideas can be found through astute observations and careful listening to the people, place, and culture. Once realized, these insights have the potential to unify design forms across scales—relating fixtures in a park, for instance, to broader contextual characteristics that reflect an authentic spirit of the community.

The following examples are but a small selection of projects demonstrating how early contextual insights are translated into final form. Since there are "no limits to scale," the projects range from broader agrarian community visions and riverfront parks to more specific elements like a stone mound and the shape of a park. At play in all of these are design characteristics that are considered in shaping the final form:

- › Texture
- › Theme
- › Tone
- › Line
- › Contrasts
- › Repetition
- › Scale
- › Counterpoint
- › Color
- › Touch and sound
- › Vista
- › Rhythm
- › Geomorphic and biomorphic design

Prairie Crossing: A Conservation Community

Greyslake, IL | c.1992 - Present
Collaborators: (see list of consultants)

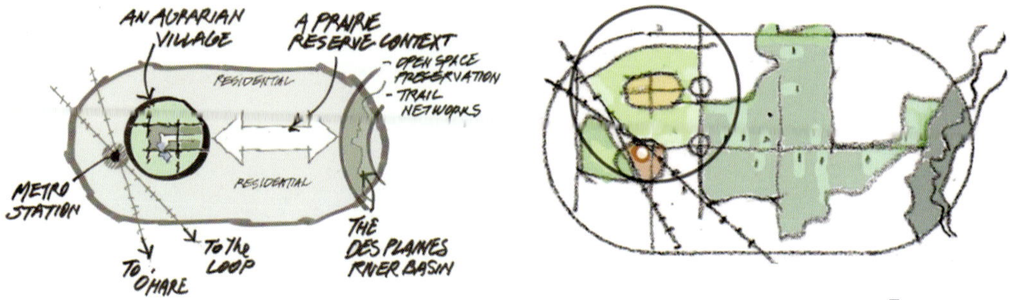

FIG. 50: Two diagrams showing the contextual considerations shaping the conservation-development direction.

These three diagrams (Fig. 50 & Fig. 51) sum up the Bones of an inspired long-term Vision ... a Conservation Community with an agrarian spirit. Note the strength of its simple forms and muted colors. The practice of seeing the whole while shaping the pieces continues to be highly relevant given increasing urban densities. And seeking to bring out the Bones can do much to increase overview insights and context awareness, and to find a delicate balance in Earth's carrying capacity while urban density and sprawl continues with few limits.

In the late 1980s, Gaylord Donnelley, a Chicago businessman of renown whose printing press bore his last name, began exploring the potential creation of a new community near Libertyville, Illinois. The intent was to develop a conservation-oriented residential community as an alternative to a major business-oriented development. Mr. Donnelley lived in the same rural area and was an advocate of wildlife and prairie restoration.

In 1990, after more than three years of planning efforts led by Vicky and George Ranney, niece and nephew of Mr. Donnelley, Prairie Crossing—a completed conservation community—was placed on the market. The plan targeted about 360 detached homes and 36 condominiums, clustered on 677 acres of open space and agricultural lands, with careful preservation. It sought to offer a quality of life, a sense of community, and a compelling alternative to another proposed development that would have seen 2,400 homes sprawled across the same site. Two rail lines crossed at the site (thus the name) with a transit station within walking distance. From that station one could travel by train to O'Hare Airport in 40 minutes and to Chicago's downtown Loop in one hour.

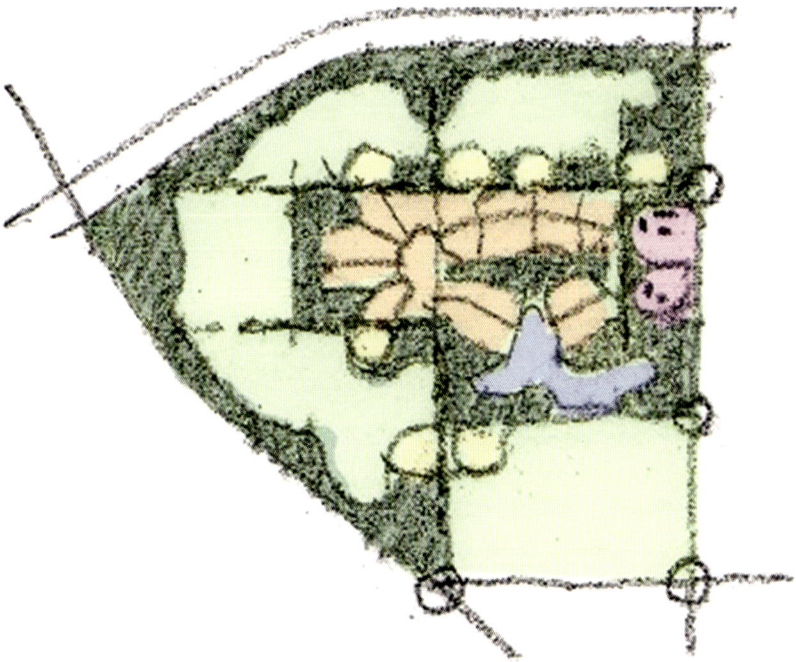

FIG. 51: Framework diagram for the Prairie Crossing development demonstrating the compact community vision balancing livability and nature preservation.

A special feature of the project is the establishment of a 5,800-acre Liberty Prairie Reserve surrounding the site based on private ownerships abiding by modest development densities and some trail access patterns, all through voluntary deed restrictions. The owners of an adjacent landfill operation were persuaded to modify their long-term processes to engineer odor controls, shape a naturalized form, and assist in funding a portion of the area-wide trail system costs. This remarkable collaboration between private landowners, residents, local government, and environmental nonprofits is the driving force behind the Vision to protect the land, safeguard the natural heritage, and support the rich ecology of Lake County, Illinois. Together, they have built and connected miles of trails, undertaken inventories, and restored various habitats.

Today, Prairie Crossing is fully built out and serves as an integrative thinking model for land development.[20] Its remarkable success stems from one person's Vision for conserving valued natural resources while accommodating development needs, each supporting the other.

It is an intentional living and learning community distinguished by these key elements:

› The homes were built with state-of-the-art construction to achieve comfort and energy efficiency.

› It is an example of a transit-oriented development with two stations serving the North Central Line to Chicago and the Milwaukee District North Line. A "Main Street" town center between the two stations serves as the entry to the village.

FIG. 52: The Byron Colby Barn and the Prairie Crossing Charter School Campus (credits: Har Ye Kan).

- The nationally recognized, award-winning Prairie Crossing Charter School provides a "learning by doing" education with a focus on the outdoors.
- Local agricultural heritage is celebrated by a 110-acre farm that supports local and north suburban Chicago markets, as well as residents who maintain a community garden plot or participate through farm shares.
- At the heart of the community is the Byron Colby Barn—a historic barn from 1885 that was carefully restored to be the gathering place; it has a fitness facility and a large events space.
- A multipurpose village green with views of the central lake and lush wetlands supports various seasonal, community, and private events.
- A system of greenways, trails, wildlife corridors, and the extensive Liberty Prairie Reserve uphold the environmental preservation goals of the community. This is managed by the Liberty Prairie Conservancy, a community nonprofit that leads habitat restoration and environmental education programs. Funding and operational support are made possible by membership dues, grants, and the Liberty Prairie Foundation.

FIG. 53: Prairie Crossing today with a mix of housing overlooking the lush wetlands and restored prairies (credits: Har Ye Kan).

Landscape Architecture & Environmental Planning Consultants:

- Steve Apfelbaum
- Geoff Deigan
- Philip Enquist, FAIA
- William J. Johnson, FASLA
- Peter Schaudt, FASLA

Architects:

- Dirk Danker
- T. Gunny Harboe, FAIA
- Walker Johnson
- Linda Keane, AIA
- Mark Keane, AIA
- Joseph Lstiburek
- Margaret McCurry, FAIA
- Jim Nagle
- Betsy Pettit, FAIA
- Frederick Phillips, FIA
- William Sturm
- Todd Wiltse, AIA

Asahikawa Downtown Expansion to the Riverfront

Asahikawa, Japan | 2000s–present
Collaborators: PWP Landscape Architecture, Nihon Toshi Sogo Kenkyusho, Hokkaido Engineering Consultants.

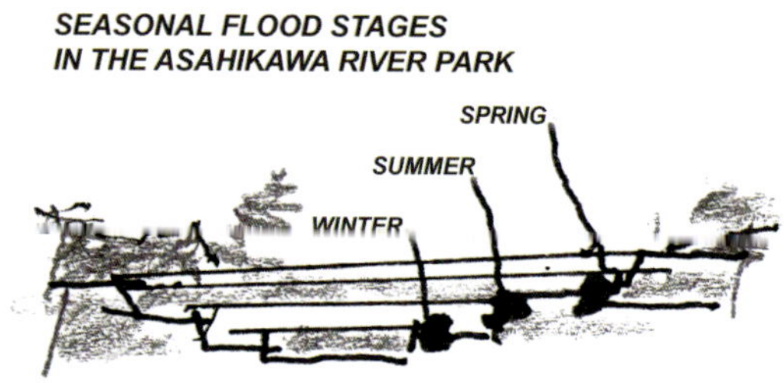

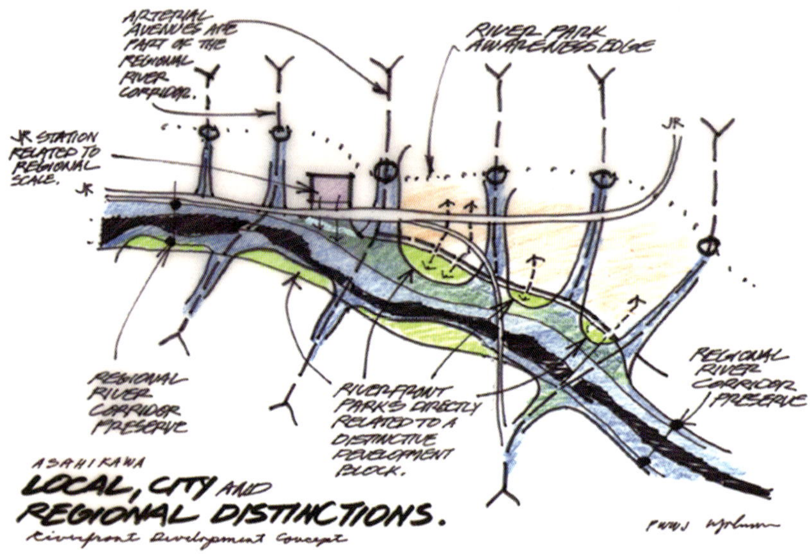

FIG. 54: Framework diagram showing the corridors connecting the central city to the Chu-Betsu River with a key arrival center at the JR Station. A series of riverfront parks terrace down to the river where native riparian vegetation at each level varies with the seasonal flood stages, creating an ever-dynamic riverfront as shown in the section.

Working with Peter Walker (Peter Walker William Johnson and Partners), Gen Kato, and Junji Goto (Japanese architects and planners), the primary task was to integrate new plans for downtown, transportation, and the riverfront, including floodplain restoration.

The River Park featured the idea of a new park outline at each of the three major flood stages.

A new transit station was the bridging function between the River Park and Downtown, which featured a mix of residential and retail. The notion that the River Park configuration intentionally changes at each flood stage was most intriguing to the residents.

Our Japanese partners were superb colleagues. They enjoyed the design process and were always thoughtful and gracious. Today, the River Park (Asahikawa Kitasaito Gardens) just behind the JR Rail Station features an impressive tapestry of textures, weaving the floodplain, terraces, and retention ponds with ribbons of paths, grasses, perennials, and annuals.

FIG. 55: Sketch of an aerial view for the Asahikawa Downtown Riverfront Vision showing penetration and awareness of the riverfront system deeper into the city.

FIG. 56: Asahikawa River Park (Kitasaito Gardens) today with its impressive landscape tapestry and site design to morph with different flood stages (credits: en.visit-hokkaido.jp).

Harima Science Garden City: A City in the Forest

Nishi Harima, Japan | 1993–present
Collaborators: PWP Landscape Architecture

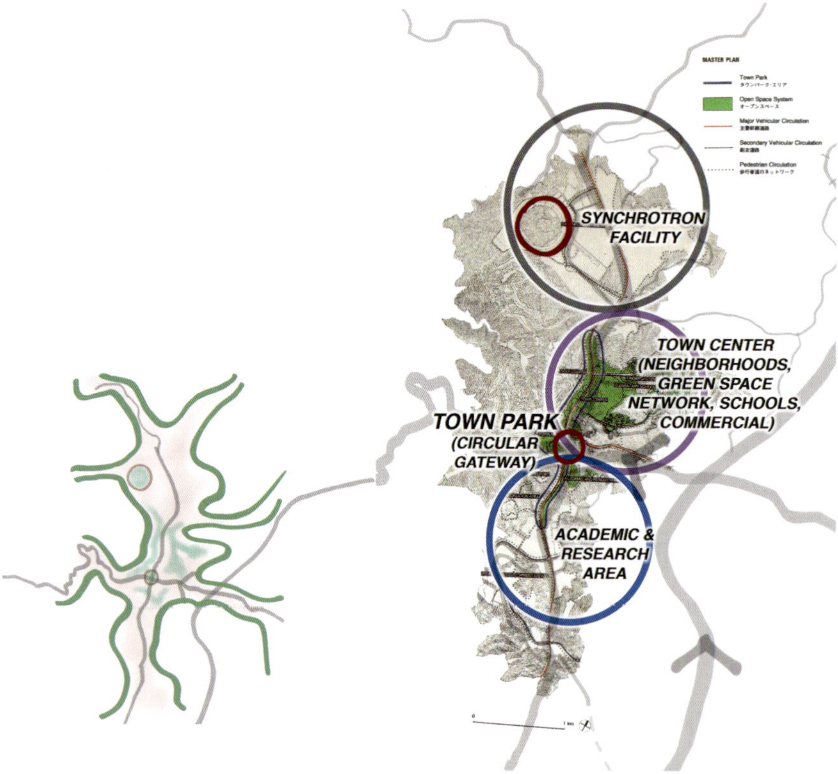

FIG. 57: Framework plan for the Harima Science Garden City: A Linear "City in the Forest." The big idea here was to "follow the corridor and there you will find the plan" (credits: PWWJ, Har Ye Kan).

In 1993, the Peter Walker William Johnson and Partners (PWWJ) office prepared a long-range master plan for a new 5,000-acre town that would house an atomic energy plant and research facility in a mountainous setting. Working in concert with this Harima Science Garden City Master Plan, Peter Walker's Stone Mound and Circle Park are examples of enduring iconic art forms. These distinctive landscape and urban design forms are crafted from contextual clues, departing from the formal geometry, "rooms," focal points, hierarchy of order, and grandeur of neoclassical Beaux-Arts gardens, parks, and forums of Rome, London, and Washington, D.C.

More importantly, both the plan and the parks demonstrate the potential of landscape architects to shape a project from macro-scale planning to micro-level design detail. In the words of Jane Gillette, "Harima proves that in the very best work these two are intimately, if not inextricably, intertwined."[21]

The town program centered around a supercollider and a branch of the Himeji Institute of Technology in a complex, volcanic formation landscape with cryptomeria groves running into pine and oak forests. The master plan sought to embrace several ideas and goals:

FIG. 58: Sketch showing the linear city form through the mountains and forests, suggesting the possibilities of living in the foothills of Japan.

- that small, remote-like development can occur on mountainous terrain, which evokes a spiritual reverence in Japanese culture.
- to knit the community through a walking and biking system.
- to highlight the strong juxtaposition between the open space systems and the automobile system.
- to "celebrate the vertical" in the integration of architecture and terrain.
- to blend "suburbanity living and a mountainous environment".[22]

Known today as Koto ("City of Light"), the community is composed of neighborhoods and a highly visible downtown connected by an integrated open space system of small parks, woodlands, and trails to preserve as much of the surrounding hilltops as possible while replanting the native forest. Techno Central Park serves as the gateway to the community its circular layout recalling the form of the supercollider. It separates and unifies the different development areas, including an institutional and research precinct, the downtown, and housing. Views are maximized and housing is clustered in pedestrian-friendly complexes perched along the hills (but not lining the roads).

Taking the contextual cues a step further on the smaller scale are the gardens designed by Peter Walker at Techno Central Park and in the Center of Advanced Science and Technology (CAST)—an homage to the mountains. Defining the town park's perimeter are karst outcrops, groves of Japanese cedar (Sugi), while a central stone mound illuminated with red light recalls the earth volcano mounds commonly found in Japan along the Pacific Ring of Fire. The mounds are repeated and expressed in a smaller, geometric form at the nearby CAST, where 35 grass cones are crowned by Skyrocket juniper trees illuminated by a red light, rigged to rise as the tree grows. They are abstracted forms representing the system of volcanoes, laid out in an orderly pattern to visually express the intellectual thought underlying the positive science and engineering spirit. In the courtyard, two larger cones rise in contrast to one another. One is covered with moss, another with

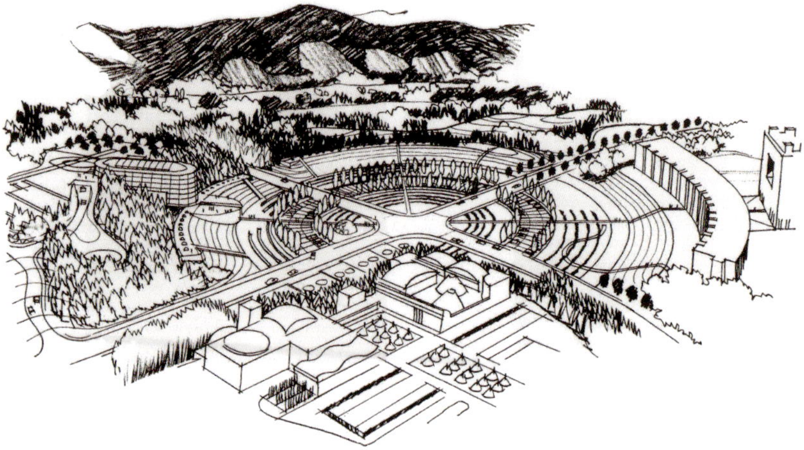

FIG. 59: The concept for the Harima Science Garden City Town Center and the completed garden forms, including the stone mounds recalling the geomorphic forms of the volcanic archipelago (credits: PWP Landscape Architecture).

riprap. Surrounded by stepping-stones that pass between the two cones, the courtyard with local blue gravel raked into circles recalls a traditional Japanese garden.

Harima Garden Science City landscape design projects thus demonstrate the unity of context, design, and form. "Community form" and "Object form" at the broader and smaller scales embody and echo a common set of design principles, ideas, and intentions. Each Object form is a piece of the whole, and because of the strong design structure giving coherence to all the pieces, the Community form becomes greater than the sum of its parts.

Garden Homes: Saving a Neighborhood

Ann Arbor, MI | 1967–present

Collaborators: Johnson, Johnson & Roy, Inc. (JJR)

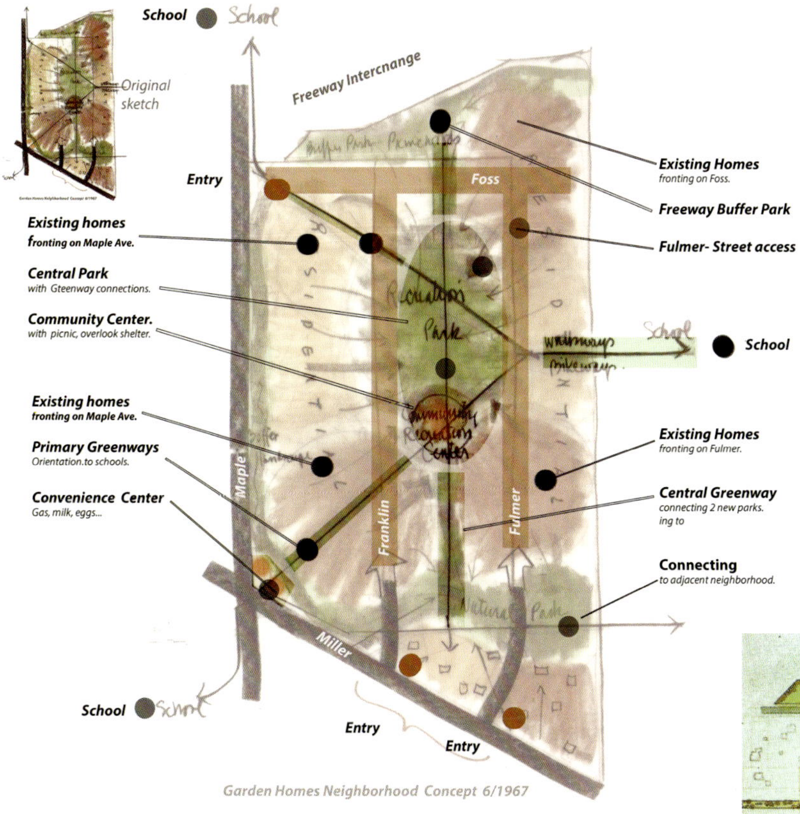

Garden Homes Neighborhood Concept - JJR 1967

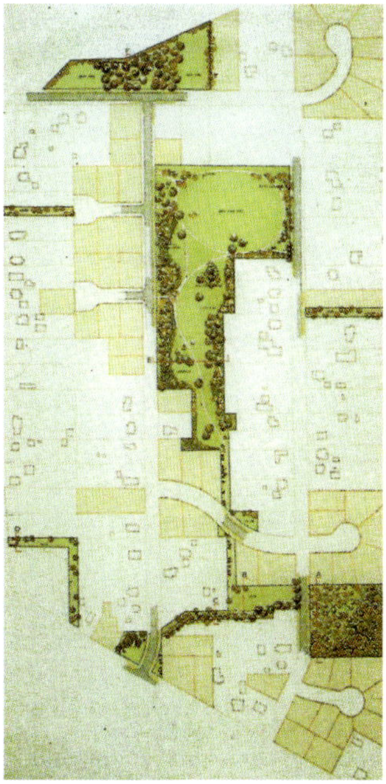

FIG. 60: Concept for the Garden Homes Neighborhood showing the proposed community center, central park, convenience corner, and central greenway, based on the children's circulation patterns and the preliminary design plan for the connected system of green spaces (credits: JJR, c. 1967).

FIG. 61: The Garden Homes Community (c. 1967) before a planning/design process was put in place based on the residents' desires to remain (credits: JJR).

FIG. 62: The Garden Homes Community today (c. 2024) (credits: Kevin Johnson).

This is a story of survival. In 1967, a well-worn 90-home neighborhood at Miller Ave and Maple Rd in Ann Arbor was the proposed location for a new shopping mall. After several months of meetings, the developer had persuaded most homeowners, one by one, to sell out. Plans were being made to clear the site. The die was cast...or was it?

During the neighborhood's last planning session, one of the members excused herself to take a walk, ending up downtown. She passed by the JJR office at Miller Ave and N. Main St about 9:00 PM, where I was working late. She took a chance and knocked on the door. In tears, she told me the story of what she called a "failure." As a small group of social workers, they had fought to keep the 90 families together, knowing firsthand that so many residents did not want to sell out. But under the intense pressure of the developer, each one was intimidated enough to agree to sell. I asked if I could get a chance to briefly meet and talk to the neighbors. Providentially, the committee meeting was still underway, and we hurried back.

The committee was then asked if they were *sure* the residents wanted to sell out to the developer. The committee said that they were quite sure that they did *not* want to sell out. The committee was further asked if the group would be willing to stick with it another week or two to see if a formal survey could confirm the community's desires. They agreed to stay active if it could be done quickly.

Grad students in the survey research program at the University of Michigan designed a confidential questionnaire, asking, "Do you want to stay, or do you want to sell?" Most residents responded in confidence, and a meeting was arranged to hear the results. The committee presented the findings of the questionnaire. Over 90 percent of those interviewed indicated they wanted to stay. Accordingly, no one sold out. That night, the residents committed to staying organized, newly motivated toward shaping a stronger community.

From this troubled beginning, a planning/design process was outlined to install sewer and water, design new streets, locate a new greenway

FIG. 63: The Garden Homes Community (c. 2024) with well-loved homes, a community park, a place of worship, and a corner commercial development (credits: Kevin Johnson).

network, design a corner retail center, redefine the Township plat, and work out a strategy for paying the bills. Within five years, all things were put in their proper place. Each year since, this mixed-use neighborhood continues to thrive, shaping a quality place to live. The discovery of the community's feature—which was the innate modesty of the place—was key to its success. In addition, what became fundamental to determining Community form in this case was the open space: the connected system of paths, greenways, a central park, and a buffer park, all working together to knit the neighborhood into a whole.

Grand Valley State University: Enduring Bones

Allendale, MI | 1960s–present
Collaborators: Johnson, Johnson & Roy, Inc. (JJR)

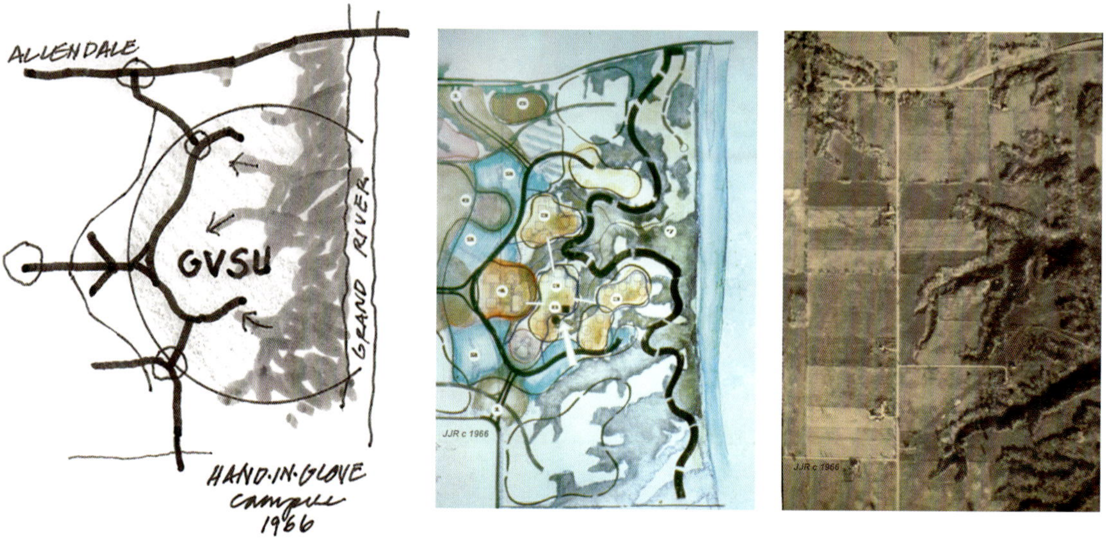

FIG. 64: Early Framework diagram and photo showing the "hand-in-glove" concept for GVSU, inspired by the deep ravines that are a prominent feature of the landscape evident in the historic aerial photograph (c. 1960s).

The name of Grand Valley State College (GVSC) was chosen after the site was selected in southwest Michigan to serve the greater Grand Rapids Area. Dr. Philip W. Buchen continued as the chief executive officer, giving form to the college programs. While a search process to hire the college's first president was being prepared, JJR was asked to prepare the initial physical planning concept.

THE EARLY JJR CAMPUS PLAN — GVSC 1966

The initial design concept for the campus was highly influenced by the deep ravine patterns extending westward into the site from the Grand River. The several plateaus formed by the ravine cuts were about 25–40 acres in size, well suited to future sub-areas of a campus. The ravines featured mature oaks and beech trees that provided an immediate sense of place to the early campus form. The early campus plan included a pedestrian bridge connecting two plateaus, where one could pass through the tops of enormous beech trees. The primary road system embraced the ravine patterns from the west, helping to blend the flat rural fields with the richness of the Grand River Valley terrain. We called it a "hand in glove fit."

Bill Kessler of Meathe-Kessler, Detroit, was part of the design team and was assigned the programming and design of the first set of buildings.

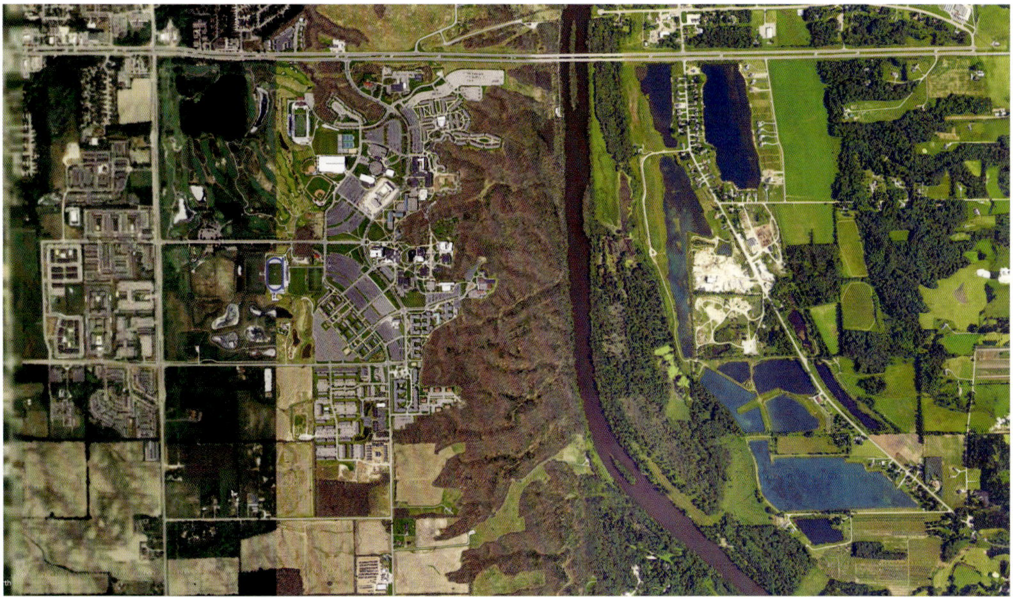

FIG. 65: Aerial of the contemporary campus layout showing the enduring Bones of the "hand-in-glove" inspiration in response to the unique ravine environment (c. 2023) (source: Google Earth).

THE GVSU CAMPUS TODAY

Since my involvement throughout the 1960s, the campus has grown well beyond any expectations I had at the time. The name shifted from "College" to "University" and branch campuses later emerged in each of the region's three metro areas. We did know, however, that the early Bones were good; a strong dose of early campus character was provided by the ravine patterns and great flexibility with the broad, open plateau to the west. Campus facilities are nestled up against these majestic forms, following the patterns of the land and then westwards of course, into the green rural fields. Carved out during the Ice Age by tributaries, the ravines are the University's most prominent features. Knitting this unique ecological environment along the Grand River with the Allendale campus is a trail system offering the community a quiet place of respite, recreation, and learning.

It is gratifying to realize that campus patterns over a 50-year period held strongly to the original hand in glove inspiration.

Downtown Holland DNA: Context-Based Design Guidelines

Holland, MI | 1960s–present
Collaborators: Gordon Van Wylen, Greg Holcombe, Søren Wolff, Phil Meyer

The efforts to revitalize Downtown Holland are a classic case of successful long-term community visioning and stewardship in mid-sized to small American cities. A vibrant community with a population of approximately 34,000 along the shores of Lake Michigan, Holland was established by Dutch immigrants in the mid-19th century. Today, it is one of the safest, most attractive places to live in the United States, with a mix of agriculture, manufacturing, tourism, healthcare, and institutional activities.

Maintaining a high quality of life has been intrinsic to the community's ethos, and Holland's charm is underpinned by careful stewardship of cherished heritage, parks, greenways, and open spaces, and its cultural diversity. This is epitomized by Downtown Holland's Vision as a connected, quality destination blending residential, commercial, campus, and waterfront uses.

A rudder for realizing shared Vision has been a strong public–private partnership built on trust among community leaders. Additionally, the postcard-perfect downtown is the result of several other action-oriented initiatives working in accord:

› Key *projects* in advancing public space improvements and private redevelopments.
› Concerted year-round *programming* to activate the community destination.
› Well-timed, significant *planning* efforts to refresh the Downtown Strategic Plan and to undertake deeper dives into smaller, more defined areas of interest (e.g., the 6th Street Corridor, Civic Center Place and Farmers' Market, and Waterfront Holland).
› Intentional city *policies* and commonly held understandings about the intended quality of the aspired outcomes.

COMMON SENSE DESIGN PRINCIPLES

The Framework diagram (See Chapter Three: Visions) is a culmination of everything that leads us in a direction, and an easy reference to take to pragmatic movers and shakers. At a smaller scale, concepts that focus on select areas offer different interpretations of development possibilities. Eventual design forms have then materialized through various public and private projects. For more than 30 years, this has steadily and surely created a sense of Main Street coherence by following the well-defined process. Unifying these forms is a set of "Downtown DNA" guidelines articulated in the Downtown Strategic Plan, a policy document to steer long-term downtown development. The essence, look, scale, and character of downtown were distilled into several fundamental common-sense principles:

› Contextual: Working with what is already here and proven while incorporating the aspirational in a neighborly way over time.
› Human scale: Blending human scale developments within the landscape scale, including the streets, pocket parks and open spaces, greenways, and the waterfront. A consistent streetscape provides a solid background to the buildings.
› Urban Design "Fit" with Appropriate Architectural Features:
  - Materials: Brick and stone on 8th Street
  - Scale: Two-story as the standard with the occasional taller buildings of three to five stories, and above six stories in selected places.
  - Pedestrian Interface: Comfortable, easy, smooth, and transparent with storefront glazing.

Extending the Vision

DOWNTOWN HOLLAND VISION - PRIORITY INITIATIVES

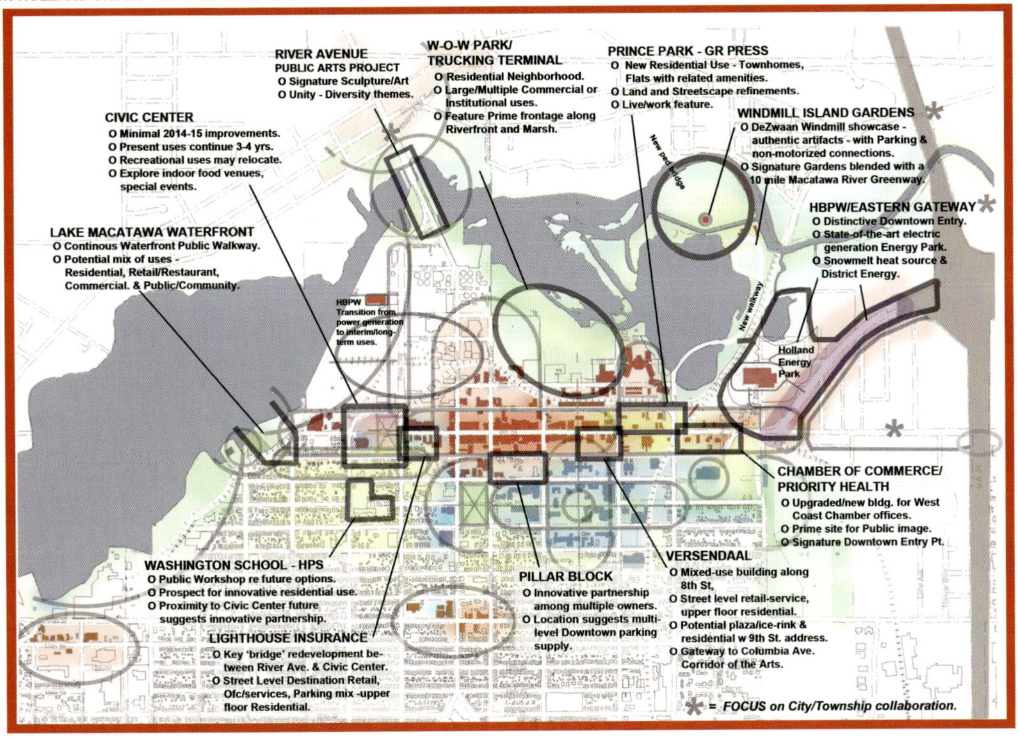

FIG. 66: Overview of priority projects within the Downtown Vision outlined in the 2015 'Extending the Vision' Strategic Plan.

- Corners: Strong, attractive, inviting, and strategic. These can serve as anchors in contrast to background or bridge buildings.
- Textures and Details: To express care and character without being too "slick," "polished," "flat," or modern.

› Marketable: Fulfills market demand and is financially sustainable over time.

› Special Landmarks: One-off exceptions for unique buildings and uses that do not establish a new precedent.

› Compatible Uses in Complementary Locations: Retail and service businesses located in ground-floor spaces; offices/non-customer-facing uses in upper floors.

Downtown Holland is distinguished by remarkable legibility and design excellence. It stems from sustained attention to the Vision and the details carried forth by many generations. It reflects pride and care by the people for the place. Above all, it is rooted in an unwavering commitment to what the

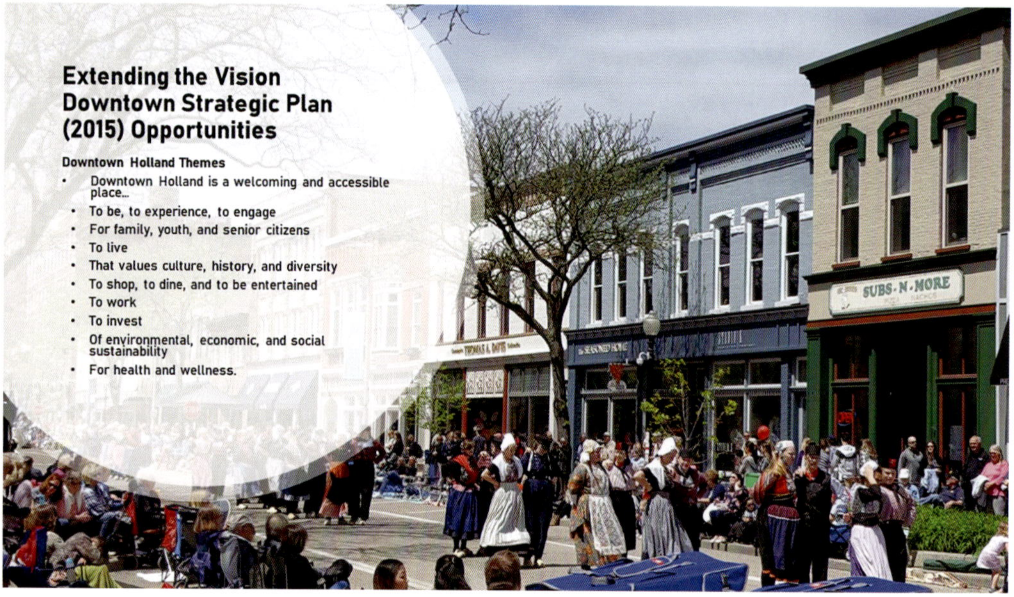

FIG. 67: Downtown Holland at Tulip Time – Dutch dance and parade along 8th Street with its carefully restored properties, quality shops, and lush streetscapes.

downtown property owners and businesses refer to as the "Holland quality."

By leaning into the community's history and character, the downtown identity and uses are framed into the place shaping, making it special, noticeable, and worthy. More importantly, the Downtown Holland DNA is also an instance of how design form and resolution can be expressed differently—not through a solo project outcome, but a carefully orchestrated, harmonious symphony of various parts and pieces, ever toggling between the macro (Vision) and the micro (practical opportunities).

Crystal Mountain: Keeping the Vision Across Generations

Thompsonville, MI | 1980s–present
Collaborators: Johnson Hill Land Ethics Studio & Joe Porter, FASLA

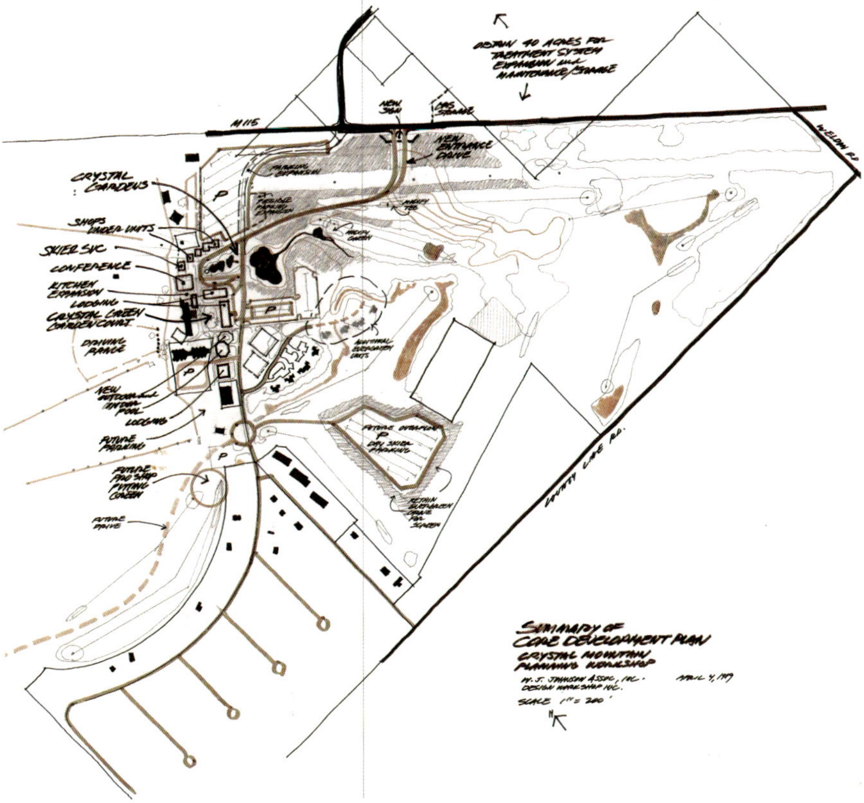

FIG. 68: Early framework diagram c. 1989 showing the core area, the opportunities, and the key early initiatives to define the resort, including a new entry road to strengthen the arrival experience by "coming out of the woods" and an indoor spa/pool facility to complement the lodge.

Crystal Mountain is a ski resort built by community in the Buck Hills range of Benzie County in northern Michigan. What started as a geography class project to determine a suitable ski area sowed the seeds of the Buck Hills Ski Club in 1956. Renamed the Crystal Mountain Resort in 1960, the club became a commercial venture and transformed into a year-round, full-service resort with winter recreation and summer activities like Ox Roast, camps, music, and golf.

FIG. 69: Portion of the 2024 Overall Master Plan showing how the various elements in the core area were realized over time, true to the early design intentions and guiding principles. (credits: Johnson Hill Land Ethics Studio)

With consolidated ownership in 1981 under the Petritz family, a new chapter of thoughtful development began.[23] In casting a long-term vision for this unique property, the "Emergent Directions" master plan was developed with Mark Johnson and Chet Hill (Johnson Hill Land Ethics Studio) to guide iterative and careful investments in creating a welcoming, pedestrian-friendly village. Joe Porter, FASLA (Design Workshop), brought his keen insights and extensive resort design experience from Colorado. Together, the team visited other ski resorts early in the process. Through their careful observations, they looked for ways to add to the existing core area while keeping the strong local character.

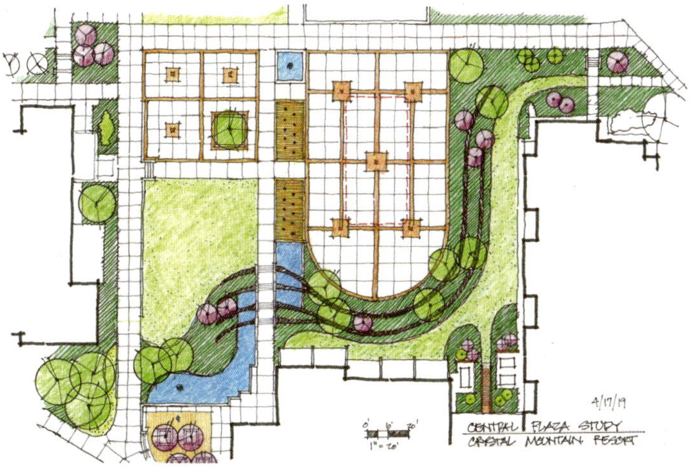

FIG. 70: Example of a detailed study for a new plaza with a conceptual plan (credits: Johnson Hill Land Ethics Studio).

FIG. 71: A sketch illustrating how this central gathering space could feel with an open area, lush plantings, and a distinctive water feature at Barr Park.

Since then, the master plan was updated at key milestones in reflecting areas of completed development and strategic opportunities for future undertakings. As the resort got to each new 'bubble' of opportunity, more detailed studies were conducted, often in the form of brief charrettes to explore the uses, design, and character. These included the creative professions as well as the in-house real estate team who have a keen sense of the market and know what works well. Visits to northwest Michigan communities and other ski resorts such as Mont-Tremblant and the Blue Mountain in Canada further informed the design elements and guiding principles.

FIG. 72: Crystal Mountain Resort's transformation from a single lodge building with a metal pole barn for the ski rental c.1989 to a year-round Northern Michigan village today. (credits: Johnson Hill Land Ethics Studio)

Throughout the resort's development, these foundational guiding principles continue to shape its form:

› Cluster development to preserve natural, open spaces and maintain the Up North character.
› Design and incrementally build a dense village that is the center of community life.
› Build with a scale that fits in – inspired by Northern Michigan architecture.
› Use indigenous, natural materials – to reflect the regional context.
› Seek simplicity of form and authenticity of styles, such as cottages with front porches, that recall our heritage.
› Integrate natural features such as rivulets and native plantings that celebrate Northern Michigan.
› Incorporate additive quality and colors.
› Take the Long View: design carefully and build a community incrementally, over time.

The spirit of collaboration and partnership in seeking the best solutions with others is expressed in the resort's design excellence, environmental stewardship, and community-oriented placemaking. These key partnerships include Michigan Legacy Art Park; Oehme, VanSweden and Clinton & Associates (now Clinton + Reis) who enlivened the landscapes with their bold, romantic garden designs; Robert Holdeman (formerly at AAI) & Mark Humitz (Cornwell Architects) who crafted the new building additions true to the spirit of the guiding principles.[24] Finally, ski consultants from SE Group and civil engineers from Mansfield Land Use Consultants rounded out the team.

FIG. 73: The Crystal Mountain Cottages and Barr Park as materialized true to the guiding principles. (credits: Johnson Hill Land Ethics Studio)

Today, Crystal Mountain is a vibrant, magical community in all seasons. Every detail from the trails to the golf courses, the cottages to the landscaping, materialized in a manner true to its vision — an exceptional endeavor for more than three decades and counting. The key to Crystal Mountain's success has been the keeping and advancing of the shared vision under the leadership of Chris (Petritz) and Jim MacInnes and their talented team. They became careful guardians of the long view while balancing the practicalities of financing the development in smaller, iterative pieces. The commitment to quality stems from their belief that if done well, the resort will naturally do well in the market.

Equally vital to the endeavor has been the continuity of a core team. The MacInnesses found good people committed to the quality of the development and design. Working closely alongside them is a multidisciplinary planning and design team: landscape architects who have been involved early, early, early in casting the "Emergent Directions" master plan and shaping the settings, and architects who are steeped in the contextual building culture. This legacy is set to continue with the current generation of outstanding leadership, John Melcher, Karyn Thorr, Kirk Davidson, and others who are deeply familiar with the resort's vision and development, and who are passionately committed to hospitality, excellence, and fun!

CHAPTER SIX

INSIGHTS: FRAMEWORK UNDERSTANDINGS

Community is formed by people inhabiting a place, belonging to the land, and sharing its fate with other life forms. It seeks to be inclusive and is defined by its physical, historical, and cultural features. These features shape what we have in common, and how we are different, resulting in communities of communities.

For us, the call to shape community—both in casting a Vision and realizing the Form-based actions—stems from an innate call to a life that is lived with others. It is a concern for *community and environmental flourishing*: a yearning for more livable and sustainable futures that extend into the areas of health, security, ecology, economy, sustenance, and connection. It is an effort to create a thriving, interactive, open, and trusting fabric of relationships amongst and between people, in harmony with the broader environs they inhabit.

Community and environmental flourishing lie at the heart of *Framework Thinking*. It is an attitude rooted in context, intertwined with creativity, and defined by the "we" and "us." And some of the most rewarding features of working with and shaping communities are discovering *new insights* about different peoples, places, and the histories—and then thoughtfully building on those understandings in envisioning a better future for the people and places they care about.

The loose, iterative structure in *Framework Thinking* is like other well-worn, successful processes in planning and design. *In writing this book, it was our hope to achieve a couple of things. First, to glean some difference*

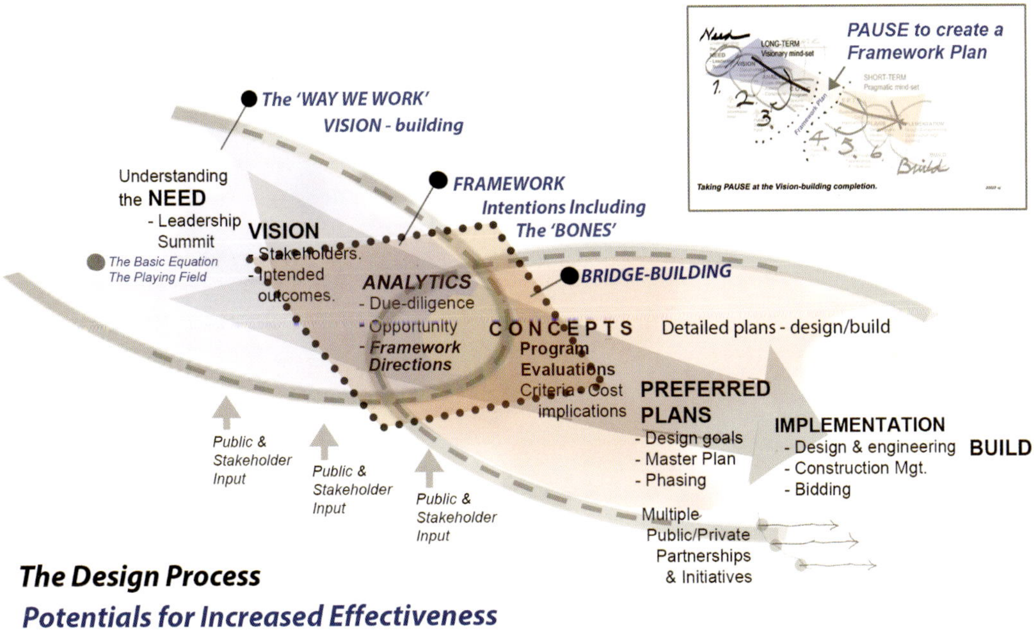

FIG. 74: Points and key "bridging" area in the planning/design process for increased effectiveness.

makers in the planning and design processes. And second, to encourage additional ways of thinking about how these creative processes could be strengthened.

Throughout our coffee talks and reflections, we were guided by this driving question: What can we do better as stewards of our communities—both people and environment—to flourish? As we come full circle, we will share what we discovered and explore where we may go from here.

The nine icons comprising the *Framework Thinking* elements are a way of approaching what otherwise are familiar planning and design processes. Together, their holistic point of view emphasizes the increased clarity, power, and enduring presence of an inspired Vision. When kept front and center in practice, the icons and Vision also accomplish several fundamentals:

(i) Finding an optimal balance between preservation needs and development interests.

(ii) Melding the strengths of multidisciplinary perspectives with multidisciplinary teams.
(iii) Providing early influence and direction grounded in robust ideation.
(iv) Telescoping between big-picture strategy and small-scale details, and between long-term considerations and short-term priorities.
(v) Articulating a Vision and direction for shaping the physical elements in a community.
(vi) Creating an enduring yet flexible Framework for various design possibilities aligned with the fundamental values and evolving needs of a community.

More importantly, as we dug deeper into our projects and reflected on what each community/client has taught us, there are three difference makers that we see as opportunities for increased effectiveness in planning and design processes. These are often the seemingly modest considerations that can turn out to be decisive in the overall quality of the outcomes.

The first are the "ways of working": to center on a Vision, to truly know the people and the place, to build ideas with others, and to keep seeing the whole even as one works with the parts. It is a purposeful search with openness and encouragement to understand the values and mindsets of who and what a community is, their roots and histories, and where they would like to go in the future.

Besides identifying the "North Star," *Vision building is an intentional approach for the beginning of the process (Visions) and the end of the process (outcomes) to be mutually informed.* Rather than discrete opposites or "either-or" entities, Visions and outcomes are more of a "both-and." By extension, the visionary and pragmatic outlooks can be two distinct yet concurrent mindsets. At times, one may tend to prevail, but both are always present, always coupled. The key, then, is how a given process can inspire participants to tap into both mindsets at the right time, to meaningfully contribute to the Vision building while grounding the directions with a healthy dose of practicality.

What we found helpful was to bring together multiple perspectives, and to involve key leaders early on who would drive a process to fruition: the project managers, construction managers, traffic and civil engineers, gardeners, and the review and regulatory personnel. When blended at the right time and in the right setting, the insights of a traffic engineer at a community charrette, or cost considerations by a construction manager in a design review, can yield more optimal, practicable outcomes.

As Rudyard Kipling sums it up powerfully: "If you can dream and not make dreams your master; if you can think and not make thoughts your aim—yours is the earth and everything that's in it."

The second is a thoughtful summation through the Framework plan and design intentions. This occurs at a *brief yet crucial moment, almost the halfway point where the big picture Framework directions begin to reveal smaller, tangible possibilities.* Here, careful attention to and a quick synthesis of the fundamental elements—the unified Vision, guiding values and principles, Framework plan, and the design and action intents—become the road map for long-term, flexible decision-making in the shaping of community.

A key part of defining the Framework is the Bones: a visual summary to convey the design intentions without defining the details and nature of the solution. These embody a Framework-oriented mindset and articulate the aspired character of a place with the principles noted. To be clear, these are expressions of long- and short-term design possibilities based on the Vision. They are not a plan and are not meant to define the nature of the solution.

There is also an art and skill to articulating the elements of Framework Thinking outcomes. Of these, the design intentions are central to mechanizing specific actions and form-based results. These are the "why" and the "what" in communicating the spirit and qualities of what the Vision is after. As they are a guiding force for seeking unity in purpose and form, the design intentions benefit from clear, timely, well-stated, and exciting descriptions. Additionally, the Bones are a vivid, easy-to-understand depiction of the big idea. What may appear as a seemingly simple diagram in fact requires deft graphical skills to know what to include, what to punch up, and how to create a lasting, compelling impression.

The time and effort to discover the Bones or the Framework is negotiable. Depending on the scale, context, and type of project, this could go very fast—and this could be a goal as well! Larger, more complicated, and publicly oriented projects may be more extensive. Conversely, the discovery phase for private initiatives with a smaller number of stakeholders may be more straightforward.

In the broader scheme of things, the duration of this early phase is often a fraction of the later phase of planning/design resolution and implementation. While relatively brief, the discovery is not to be rushed, because there are dangers in summarizing prematurely before the complexities are known. Getting the pace and duration just right becomes an exercise in leadership. Figuring out when to step in, how to lead, who to engage, how to get the momentum going with many different parts, and when to sum up are all process leadership "muscles" to build.

The third, and probably the most crucial of the three, is bridge building. The tipping point in a good process is where the transformational mindset overlaps with the pragmatic, transactional outlook: the bridging between the Vision and action, the big picture and the minutia, the people and place. It is also the most vulnerable point where competing interests are manifest, compromises are often made, and where clear, strategic decision-making is most needed.

And it is this essence of bridging that sums up Framework Thinking's overarching premise. In our professional capacities, we are not just the planners and the designers. We are the bridges and the bridge builders—the conduits, intermediaries, and facilitators. By setting in motion the understandings, process, discovery, and resolution, we build bridges:

- among people,
- within and between places,
- across different ideas, values, and mindsets,
- from needs, Visions, to outcomes,
- through the past, present, and future.

We craft the conditions in which the listening, understanding, imagining, and doing can occur with the client-community... and for the good of the client community. These conditions are a blend of analytics, creativity, and culture—the people, leadership, ideas, as well as the way we encourage others to participate and see more. These conditions are also informed by an awareness of the genius loci—the qualities, experience, and spirit

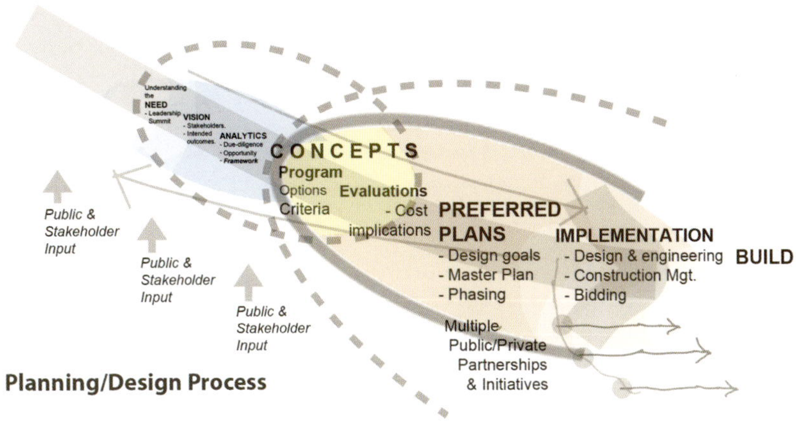

FIG. 75: Typical time and effort in the planning/design process where it is more modest in the earlier phase of Visioning and Bridge Building, and more intensive in the later phase of practical implementation.

of the place. This genius loci is ever present in the land, its forms and features, skylines and shorelines, the soils, the smells, the seasons, the views, the pulse and interactions of life, and how the layered histories of a community are articulated.

Enabling others to see more and to expect more, though, is not all sunshine and roses. There are difficult conversations to navigate. Sometimes, it is to reconcile diverging client and community interests. Other times, it is to hold leadership accountable to a Vision that has been cast and needs to be advanced. Then, there are the situations where funding, regulatory, or time limitations call for some additional creativity and resourcefulness. Or to gently recall the north star—the why—when the going gets tough on the team.

In essence, Framework Thinking is a purposeful bridge building to a preferred, inspiring future of possibilities by framing the foundational elements into a clear, unifying whole. It begins by bringing people together and helping them value each other's humanity. By fostering constructive dialogue and planting the seeds of connection, we can create a space for understanding the interdependent and holistic nature of community.

The keyword here is trust, which hinges on relationships and the ability of the bridge to remain neutral amid the myriad interests. It is not to be advocates of a plan but simply of process. In setting the table for community Visioning and flourishing, bridge builders affirm, support, establish a sense of security for people to walk together with greater courage and conviction.

EPILOGUE

BRIDGE BUILDING & NEW LEARNINGS

Going forward, we believe that the difference makers suggested in *Framework Thinking* still apply. They continue to enhance the effectiveness of any given problem-solving process—their integrative, intentional approach enables communities to flourish.

Even as we face an indeterminate future, in some ways it feels like we are seeing the cycles of history unfold. We are still grappling with many of the same issues since the 1960s, which revolve around immediate community needs and broader societal concerns. Some are longstanding challenges while others reflect brief constraints.

Today, the same issues have intensified at the local and global scales in new and different settings. It appears that even in the 21st century, our creative problem-solving endeavors within the placemaking professions remain centered on the *essence of the Basic Equation: finding a workable balance between place and people, conservation and development, wellbeing and growth.*

The goals of the Basic Equation are also surprisingly similar. What is the essence of the bigger picture? How can we engender a sense of belonging? How can we create a comingling of enriching experiences, encounters, and relationships? How can the places we craft be ones the community will love and be proud of in the generations to come?

Framework Thinking offers an opportunity to take a step back from the day-to-day and return to the fundamentals of how we can better serve the

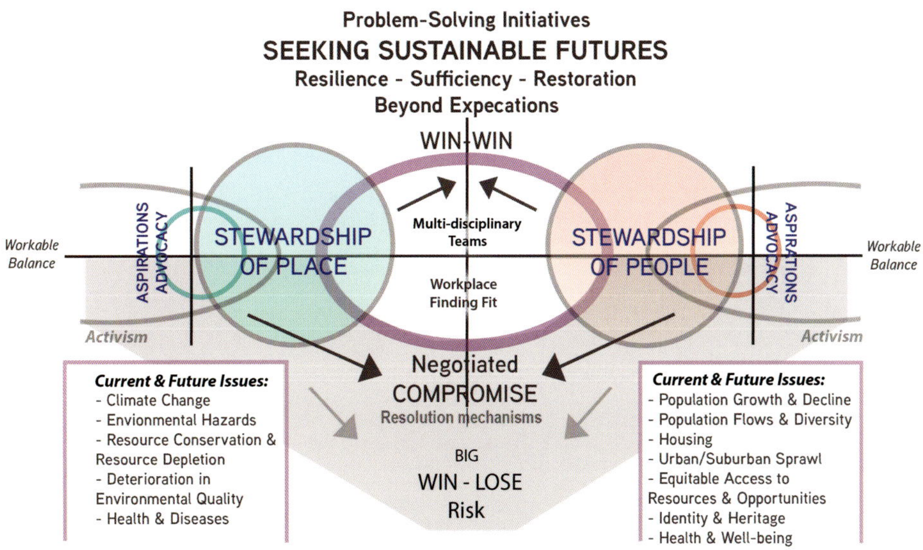

An overview of the Multi-Disciplinary Workplace in designing environmentally sensitive places of distinction.

FIG. 76: The Basic Equation amidst the current and future issues to address in the stewardship of place and community.

people and places of any given community. All nine of this book's icons nudge us toward a more mindful practice in helping others:

- See more, think big and small, and build and advance a collective Vision.
- Discover the unique qualities and Bones of a place from which other design ideas emerge.
- Set up a solid Process, which then becomes a vehicle to achieve extraordinary results.

This third point about achieving the extraordinary is a major one. Accommodating human needs and development may be accompanied by diminishing environmental quality. Contrary to this norm, what is inherently unique about *Framework Thinking* is an expectation to enhance the environment *because of* human needs and development. Instead of juxtaposing them with each other, the best outcomes *integrate* environmental preservation and development; neither one is overlooked or undervalued.

This interdependency of people and place can yield unexpected environmental performance outcomes: prairie restoration, forest conservation, water quality improvements, urban heat mitigation, biodiversity enrichment, and opportunities to connect humans and nature. Amidst this common thread to discover a fit in the relationship between people, their environment, and technology, a key question is how practitioners of landscape architecture, planning, urban design, and architecture are regarded as professionals in the practice arena.

- How do they hold their points of view even amidst the cultural challenges of the current context?
- How does the focus remain on mutually respectful, interdisciplinary problem-solving without getting swept into disciplinary critiques and political polarization?
- How does this shape education, research, and practice in preparing mindsets to embrace current and future issues with professional competency?

It appears there needs to be more encouragement of the disciplines and professional practice to hold their place with related problems circling around them ... to continue to *practice with integrity and excellence* while prizing environmental interests in the broadest sense.

As we reflect on *Framework Thinking* with an eye toward the future, we would like to offer some closing thoughts for consideration.

Stewardship, "Place Shaping," and "Place Keeping"

One of the most striking features of *Framework Thinking* is the enduring power of a shared Vision—how it propels a sense of stewardship. It involves care for and responsible management of the resources and people that have been entrusted to us, with a view to enhancing health, wholeness, and resilience.

Stewardship also suggests a broadening from "place shaping" to "place keeping." Place shaping, or more commonly referred to as placemaking, is a collaborative, multi-sector, participatory, inspirational process of community visioning and development. It is a process that builds on a community's strengths, values, and potential to create quality spaces that contribute to the people's health, happiness, and wellbeing. For us, place shaping (instead of place making) suggests a softer, facilitative role in helping the community give form to what they cherish. *Place keeping* is the long-term, active care of a place and its people, after high quality spaces—especially public ones—are created.[25]

Both the shaping and stewardship of places (place shaping and place keeping) are a labor of intentionality and openness. They depend on a holistic approach, strong partnerships, effective leadership, and a commitment to advancing a common Vision. Often, this is best sustained by a local keeper of Vision who knows the people and place or is supported by local partners. *Ultimately, community building is not a corporate endeavor but a highly relational mission.*

An example of an enduring Vision based on long-term place shaping and place keeping is the Holland Downtown Vision (see Chapter Three: Visions and Chapter Five: Resolution). Since it was first cast in the 1980s through an intentional public-and-private-sector leadership group, the Vision has been advanced and sharpened. The comprehensive plan for the economic and historic revitalization of Downtown Holland first undertook an extensive Main Street streetscape improvement program, including the installation of the country's first snowmelt system for heated public sidewalks.[26] This innovative infrastructure catalyzed various public and private sector investments and quality development projects.

Downtown Holland today is a vibrant, pedestrian-friendly, year-round destination where tree-lined streets and pocket parks and plazas co-mingle with a mix of places to live, work, dine, shop, and gather. Beyond the 8th Street spine, the downtown is connected to an extensive park and greenway system, the Hope College and Western Theological Seminary campuses, historic neighborhoods, industries, and the Lake Macatawa waterfront. The city has the largest municipally run snowmelt system in North America.[27]

In the decades since the revitalization effort was launched in the 1980s, the Vision has been implemented and refreshed at key points in

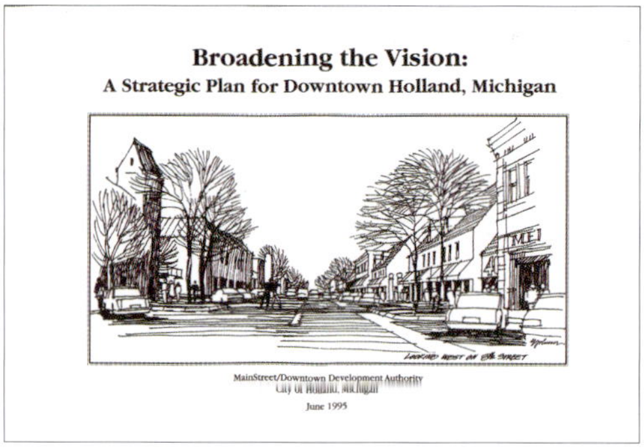

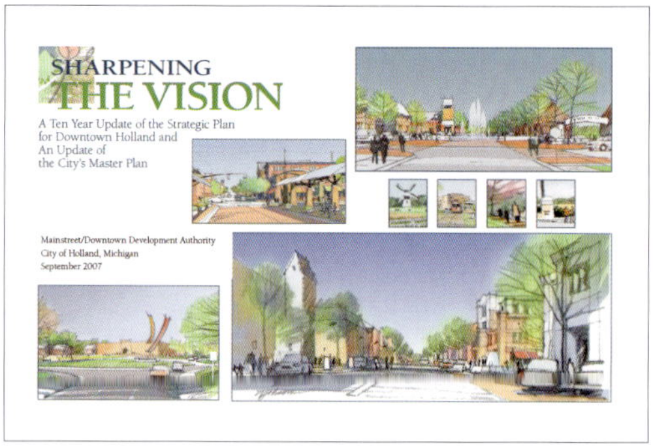

the City of Holland's development. The purposeful revisiting, refreshing, and refining of the Vision, coupled with the sustained action that constitutes 90 to 95 percent of the community-building work,[28] is what lies at the heart of place keeping. In US President Dwight Eisenhower's words, "Plans are worthless, but planning is everything ... The reason it is so important to plan is to keep yourselves steeped in the character of the problem that you may one day be called upon to solve—or to help to solve."[29]

The inspirational strategy based on a shared way of working, a commitment to excellence, and a collaborative civic stewardship for the greater good has invigorated the Holland community. Its story continues to unfold, honoring the firm foundation with an eye to the future.

Professional Performance: Advocacy and Activism

New problem-solving approaches could also emerge as the planning and design professions turn their attention to broader concerns. Some may draw on scientific methods and policy discussions, such as the exploratory projects in the Green New Deal Superstudio initiative undertaken by the Landscape Architecture Foundation and allied institutions. Others may

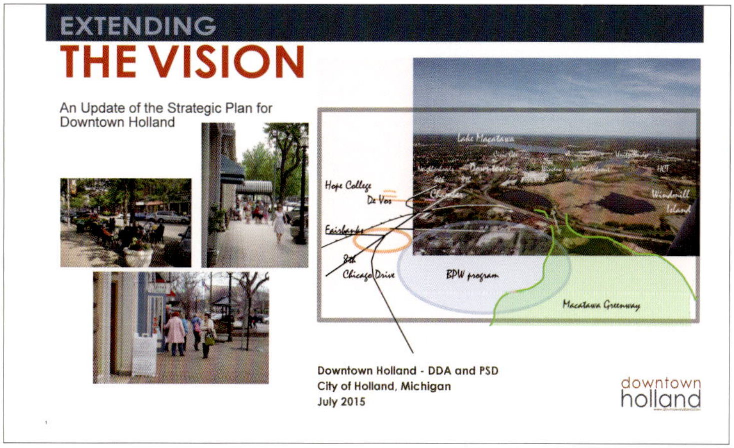

FIG. 77: Downtown Holland Strategic Plans (1995, 2007, 2015): The purposeful implementation, advancement and refinement of a strong Vision over four decades and more in Downtown Holland.

be influenced by history, new social movements, and technology, such as artificial intelligence (AI), which has profound implications on the creative process.

At the core of these new problem-solving approaches is the question of professional performance. The growing pattern of taking environmental and social issues into the political arena risks a precipitous slide from professional performance into advocacy and full-on political activism. *Advocacy* is the recommendation of and public support for an idea, belief, cause, or way of doing things. *Activism*, on the other hand, is a direct, vigorous, noticeable action to achieve a political and/or social agenda, especially in strong support of or opposition to one side of a controversial issue.

Planning and design professionals can and do incorporate advocacy in problem-solving processes; they can also respond creatively to issues articulated by activists. Rarely, if ever, do planning and design professionals find themselves operating as activists.

Within this continuum of advocacy, activism, and core professional competency, it matters a great deal how we communicate—verbally and visually—with different interest groups, and how they communicate with one another. A subtle shift from advocacy to activism, or a misperception of the advocacy process as activism, could have unintended consequences. For example, efforts by some professions to advance zoning reforms for

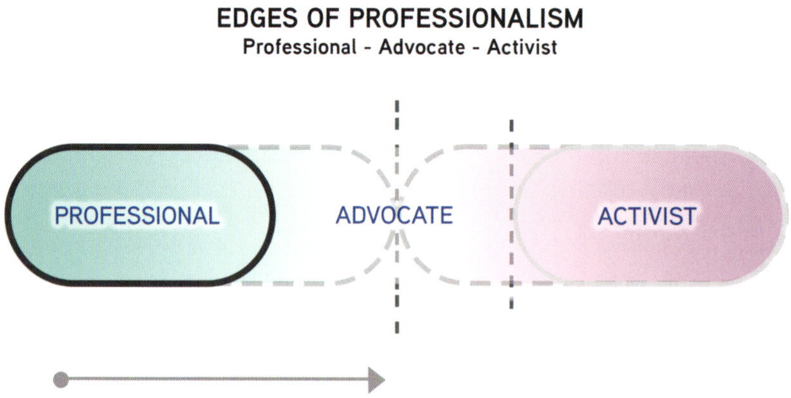

FIG. 78: Professional performance extending into advocacy, where appropriate, while remaining distinct from activism.

affordable housing development are often met with strong community reservations. Instead of seeking a middle-ground approach, if professions turn to YIMBY (Yes In My Back Yard) movements, they run the risk of slipping from advocacy to activism, potentially deepening the fractures in a community.

Similarly, developing interdisciplinary professional capabilities to work at the intersections most critical to environmental adaptation and hazard mitigation are only as effective as one's ability to engage with diverse perspectives and people on these issues. Whether one is engaged in dialogue about construction, transportation, development, land use, preservation, or restoration, when partisan slogans or terms of the times slip in, it can build barriers instead of bridges.

In the face of AI, planning and design exploration has the potential to be rapidly shortened and fundamentally transformed. Visualization tools can quickly generate creative possibilities and enhanced renderings; sophisticated data processing models can unlock and evaluate design options based on defined parameters; documentation and drafting applications can accelerate project timelines through nimble adjustments.

Amidst this technological shift, AI's efficiency gains are likely to exceed what planning, design, and the allied professions may be able to achieve in the realm of data processing and visual communication. Possibilities generated by AI, however, are still dependent on patterns, prior knowledge, and factors determined by higher-order human decisions.

Looking ahead, the planning, design, and their allied professions have an even more vital role to play in synthesizing and imagining an unpredictable future, while knowing full well that the outcomes of a plan/design do not determine how things will unfold. This role entails:

- *Understanding the context* of what a client/community is seeking to achieve, including historical, cultural, socio-political, environmental, and personal influences that are not always quantifiable or static.
- *Reviewing, verifying, and winnowing the initial possibilities* produced by AI's algorithmic permutations and combinations (which are inevitably fallible).
- *Thinking literally "outside the box" and outside the defined parameters* which may limit the creative options generated by AI. The complementary skills of critical thinking and creative thinking, which go hand in hand with innovation, rely on seeing more, making unexpected connections, and arriving at potential solutions from completely different angles.
- *Facilitating the human-centered interactions of decision-making and problem-solving.* Nuances and relational dynamics unfold in real time. These involve adroit reading of situations and the interpretation of implicit information to foster meaningful dialogue toward a satisfying resolution.

Above all, the planning and design professions have an ethical responsibility for improving relationships and asking questions that can steer conversations toward deeper understandings around which successful solutions can be crafted. Professional performance and effectiveness stem from the intermediary role that planners and designers play in community shaping processes: to be in the middle working through the healthy tension between possibilities and pragmatics, aspirations and actions. It is also a role enabled by spatial language tools such as diagramming, collage, visual surveys, and possibilities offered by AI. All of these are integral in helping a client/community feel more confident in decision-making as they tackle difficult, complex stewardship issues.

New Learnings in Process Leadership

Amidst the shifts toward shaping more livable, sustainable futures, it is even more of a challenge than ever before to create a constructive, contextually sensitive, and thoughtful approach. In a polarized cultural context, how can we hear and sift through a myriad of voices? How can we help each other see what we have in common?

In the search for creative possibilities that fit with the community context, there may be a new kind of learning in planning and design leadership. On one hand, we are learning about "others"—the ways of the community, the people and place we serve. Often, in a short period of time we must quickly develop an assessment of the physical strengths and opportunities, a sensitive grasp of the local culture and temperaments, and a keen understanding of the programing intentions.

- Who are we serving?
- How do we relate?
- What are the community's values?
- Where might we find common ground?
- How can we build on the common ground?

On the other hand, we are also learning about ourselves—the ideas and values we bring and where those are in relation to the community context.

As we worked together on this book and pondered how we wished we and future generations of planning and design professionals could be better equipped as leaders, we realized that what we were seeking goes beyond knowledge and skills. These can be acquired or deepened through practice and exposure. Instead, *we were hoping for a new kind of learning centered on the cultivation of attitudes—dispositions that are a matter of mind, person, and place.*

With today's evolving challenges regarding places and communities, the first step in process/design leadership often needs to be learning to adjust an attitude and a frame of mind. It is a soft yet enduring kind of leadership, quietly sustaining the process, the people, the discovery, and the drive to action.

To this end, we would like to offer three simple reflections that encapsulate what we have learned and continue to strive for daily, and to do so in relation to the nine icons that have served as a foundation for community building. These "learnings" or attitudes may not be new to you, but it is nevertheless helpful to explore the range of their significance. We hope that they can complement the broadly accepted, familiar qualities in the professions: empathy, excellence, innovation, and collaboration.

- *Humility:* Learning to Listen / Understanding the Community and the Professions
- *Hospitality:* Learning to Welcome / Embracing People and Honoring Ideas
- *Agility:* Learning to Adapt / Staying Nimble and Flexible

HUMILITY
Learning to Listen

> *"Listening exceeds by far the sense of hearing. Everything in us listens, because everything in the world and of the world speaks."*
> —Jean-Louis Chrétien, *The Call and the Response*

The starting point for humility is a general orientation in daily life in which the needs of others, and of the whole, are honored and kept foremost in the hearts and minds of those who serve. In simple terms, as framed by psychologist Daryl Van Tongeren, humility is to "know yourself, check yourself, and go beyond yourself."[30]

Keen self-awareness or "listening"—knowing one's own strengths, weaknesses, skills, life experiences, values, and lenses—enables one to be porous, vulnerable, and rooted in healthy growth and improvement. On a Playing Field of multidisciplinary teams and diverse community settings, self-awareness becomes a regulatory feature. It reveals the limits of each profession and perspective, encourages leaning on each other's strengths, and shares praise and wins with others.

Taking self-awareness and self-regulation one step further toward humility is an openness to accept constructive comments and responsibility. This is particularly vital in the problem-solving process, which has multiple feedback loops towards achieving excellence. In the spirit of seeking improvements, one can thus exercise conscious choices to frame and interpret questions and comments as suggestions rather than as critiques.

Lastly, humility is marked by a focus on the needs of others. A humble life is a self-offering life "open to others like a seed that opens to its soil environment by extending roots that receive and give nurture in return."[31] It is attuned and responsive to listening, seeing, and relating to people and place.

The bridge building work of shaping communities begins from the premise that the client-community bring with them a wealth of lived experiences, challenges, hopes, and aspirations. When invited to partake in a client-community's journey, our role is to immerse, absorb, and come alongside them so that their needs and potential are made evident, and the community is energized to fully become who and what it was created to be.

HOSPITALITY

Learning to Welcome

In the planning, design, and development professions, the term "hospitality" may not always be a conscious or innate mindset during a problem-solving process. What we would like to suggest is a consideration of *hospitality as a generous, friendly, warm, and welcoming disposition. We make room for others by offering safe, open, and inviting environments.* More importantly, hospitality is an act and a process of fostering positive connections, of transforming strangers into friends.

Along with humility, hospitality is a way of creating an easy setting where dialogue can be gently stimulated. It includes attention to small things to honor the broader stories and identities that intersect in collaborative planning processes. It can include, for example, learning and remembering individual names and stories, having name tags, minimizing language barriers, serving light refreshments, setting up round tables for more intimate discussions, and considering how participants of all ages and abilities can be a part of the conversation. (It is also important that good coffee is served at events!)

Hospitality is also about being fully present and fully available to the call and needs of others. To be hospitable is to listen actively, to learn the language that people use in the given place in their daily lives, to read body language, and to support moments of vulnerability so that courageous conversations can occur. In essence, it is about *establishing a heart–mind–soul connection with others: sensing the context cues, feeling the energy in the room, and fostering new understandings by building ideas together.* As Brené Brown puts it eloquently in *Atlas of the Heart*, "Language shows us that naming an experience doesn't give the experience more power, it gives us the power of understanding and meaning."[32]

By communicating with grace, compassion, creativity, and loving firmness when it is needed, hospitality is vital in working through relational dynamics and discovering the common grounds for a community to create their future together.

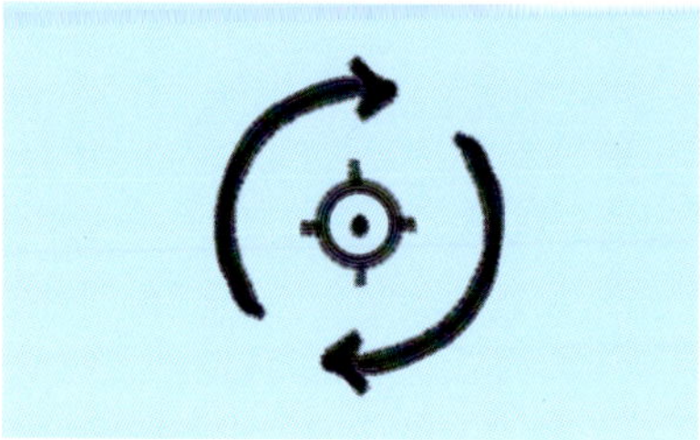

AGILITY
Learning to Adapt

Place shaping and place keeping are structured yet improvisational activities. They are dynamic processes, open to relationships, rhythms, and responses intertwined with the vibrant union of people, places, and systems. Being agile is also inherent in the spirit of learning and discovery.

Since each problem-solving process has its share of twists and turns, what matters is how they are navigated. With astute acceptance, clear-sightedness, and an open mind, bridge builders can make deft alterations so that the purpose of shaping community can continue moving toward where it was intended to go.

In the early 2020s, the COVID pandemic showed how the shaping of community can be susceptible to abrupt, unexpected shifts. When community life and gathering in person came to a standstill because of this global health crisis, public meetings, open houses, design workshops, and studios quickly shifted online to optimize stakeholder participation. We learned to Zoom, create online engagement platforms, and collaborate at a distance in highly digital environments.

Similarly, when prejudice came to a tipping point in the United States in the early 2010s and 2020s, our design and planning professions reckoned with how practices of the past led to segregation in the built and natural environments. Professional associations and schools promptly responded by reevaluating their positions and approaches, as well as their commitments to involve community members in design processes, decision-making, and outcomes.[33]

In the process of shaping community, every phase calls for flexibility. Conversations flow and evolve dynamically, new ideas and directions emerge through sketching and collective brainstorming, and site tours and outdoor engagements are at the mercy of the weather. As process leaders, how we choose to react, and pivot can set the tone for how participants respond. As the philosopher Epictetus observed, "We cannot choose our external circumstances, but we can always choose how we respond to them."[34]

Onward Together

We are one small part in a bigger, broader web of stewards in the shaping of communities. Just as a bridge is dependent on its piers, our bridge building role relies on the very residents who are part of a community's everyday life, on a community's leadership, on allied professionals, and on a perceptive grasp of the community's context. Every part matters to the whole.

When we are invited to journey with a community, it is a gift and a responsibility. It is not just a project or an assignment. To us, it is an honor to come alongside them, listen to their stories, see the world through their eyes, and enable them to discover the potential that lies within as they shape a flourishing community.

Framework Thinking is a physically oriented, design-version of strategic planning. While its formal outcomes are confined within limited bounds, its prominence lies in understanding the contextual potential, searching for the broader impacts, and thinking about the long-term implications of how each successful bridge that is crossed will enable others to fall into place.

As we contemplate current and future issues, we will need more bridge people with a mindset of learning to reveal qualities that are needed and understood by all of us. We can show up by embracing the unexpected with curiosity and kindness. We can opt for the bigger picture view by looking for possibilities rather than being confined by the parameters. We can learn to think on our feet, turning shared challenges into clarifying insights and opportunities for reconciliation ... all while keeping the community's desired values and the overarching goals of the process front and center in any tweaks that are made.

Together, may we continue building bridges, in our own small ways, for the common good. And this collective stewardship starts from within each of us. We all can cultivate the capacity to think a little more broadly, look a little further, expect a little more, and be open to an integrative, "both-and" mindset with room for both the visionary and the pragmatic, and doing so will enable us and our clients to achieve purposeful, transformational outcomes for community flourishing.

JOHNSON, JOHNSON & ROY, INC. (JJR): AN OVERVIEW

In 1961, William (Bill) Johnson formed Johnson, Johnson & Roy, Inc. (JJR) with his brother, Carl Johnson, and their friend Clarence Roy. Early in their landscape architecture careers, the kindred spirits believed that good design and good planning were mutually integrated. Together, they embraced the notion of focusing on the character of the land to discover its essence, and to strengthen its gentle symbiotic relationship with human and cultural interactions.

The complementary blend of talents was providential. Carl Johnson brought his love for plants and his unique artistic talents. Clarence Roy contributed his business acumen, strong organizational skills, and continual mentorship in the practice. Bill Johnson had an exceptional ability to stimulate creative dialogue across a broad group of stakeholders through sketching. He also brought Vision and innovation to the Ann Arbor-based firm by pushing the boundaries of landscape architecture. Bill encouraged its learning of and leaning on corollary fields such as civil engineering, environmental science, art and humanities, sociology, and urban planning.

The seeds of this collaboration were sown when Bill taught a course on understanding land use patterns at the University of Michigan. The compelling discussions soon paved the way for a comprehensive land use plan for the Central Campus, commissioned by the Board of Regents in 1963. What came from this was a campus master plan for the University of Michigan. This first project also led to the firm's innovative

FIG. 79: Carl Johnson, Clarence Roy & Bill Johnson (c. 1967) (credits: The Cultural Landscape Foundation).

Framework approach that became widely adopted in the planning and design professions in the form of the Framework plan.

It was a big-picture view grounded in analytics and a strong understanding of the interdependency between the natural and human systems. Besides physical features such as the open space elements, drainage patterns, topography, and views, cultural factors were equally important to discern. This included history, things people valued, special events, and the character and feel of a community.

The Framework approach yielded a flexible plan expressed as the Bones of a place—a structure within which buildings, uses, and developments become further defined at the opportune time before moving into implementation. Because of its enduring quality in guiding long-term development, JJR's unique Framework approach spurred the firm's impressive growth through the 1960s and 1970s.

Steeped in a strong Midwestern tradition of naturalism, community, and a sensitivity to the context, Johnson, Johnson & Roy, Inc. (JJR) became one of the most respected interdisciplinary firms in North America. From a small, three-man team, it grew to a firm of more than 30 people and merged with Smith, Hinchman & Grylls (SHG, later SmithGroup) in the early 1970s. By the 1980s and into the 1990s, the JJR client base came from across the United States, Europe, and the Middle East. The firm had multiple offices in Ann Arbor, MI, Dallas, TX, Chicago, IL, and Madison, WI. In 2000, JJR incorporated and became SmithGroupJJR. Today, the firm continues as part of SmithGroup.

Bill Johnson retired from the firm in 1975 to become the dean of the School of Natural Resources at the University of Michigan. Carl Johnson retired in 1989, followed by the final founding father, Clarence Roy in 1992.

JJR's environmental stewardship, sustainability, interdisciplinary thinking, collaboration, creative discovery, and contextual design are undoubtedly the marriage of planning and design par excellence. Its legacy is epitomized in the timelessness and true sense of place in the communities and projects they crafted.

Selected JJR Projects

Academic Campuses

- Goshen College, Goshen, IN
- Grand Valley State University, Allendale, MI
- Indiana University, Bloomington, IN
- Kentucky State University, Frankfort, KY
- Michigan Technological University, Houghton, MI
- Northern Michigan University, Marquette, MI
- Penn State University, State College, PA
- University of Connecticut, Storrs, CT
- University of Michigan, Ann Arbor, MI
- University of Wisconsin-Madison, Madison, WI
- Valparaiso University, Valparaiso, IN
- Western Kentucky University, Bowling Green, KY

Sustainable Environments

- Crosswinds Marsh, New Boston, MI
- Franconia Notch, White Mountains, NH

- Garden of the Gods, Colorado Springs, CO
- Lost Dog Wash and Gateway Trailheads, McDowell Sonoran Desert Preserve, Scottsdale, AZ
- Pictured Rocks National Lakeshore, MI
- Guidelines for tourism recreation in Michigan's Upper Peninsula, MI

Cities
- Ann Arbor downtown, Ann Arbor, MI
- AT&T Center for the Performing Arts, Dallas, TX
- Fort Collins downtown redevelopment, Fort Collins, CO
- W. K. Kellogg Foundation, Battle Creek, MI

Communities
- Franklin Village, Franklin, MI
- Garden Homes, Ann Arbor, MI
- Kellogg Headquarters, Battle Creek, MI
- The Homestead, Leelanau, MI

Waterfronts
- Chicago lakefront, Chicago, IL
- Cleveland lakefront, Cleveland, OH
- Detroit riverfront, Detroit, MI
- Forest Park Beach, restoration, Lake Forest, IL
- Milwaukee downtown waterfront, Milwaukee, WI
- Northerly Island, Chicago, IL
- Traverse City waterfront development and downtown revitalization, Traverse City, MI

Historic Preservation
- C. S. Mott Estate restoration, Flint, MI
- Highland Park, MI
- Historic preservation inventory, Grand Rapids, MI
- Marshall Plan for preservation, Marshall, MI

Endnotes

1 Walker, Peter and Melanie Simo, *Invisible Gardens: The Search for Modernism in the American Landscape.* Cambridge, MA.: MIT Press, 1994. 216.

2 William J. Johnson Oral History Transcript. Conducted by Charles A. Birnbaum, The Cultural Landscape Foundation, August 25–28, 2015: https://www.tclf.org/sites/default/files/atoms/files/Bill%20Johnson%20Oral%20History_Transcript_DRAFT_05JAN_0.pdf, 65–66.

3 Ibid., 68.

4 Doris Kearns Goodwin, *Leadership in Turbulent Times* (New York: Simon & Schuster, 2018), 234–35.

5 Lance Brown, David Dixon, and Oliver Gilham, *Urban Design for an Urban Century: Shaping More Livable, Equitable, and Resilient Cities* (San Francisco: John Wiley & Sons, 2014); Peter Newman, Timothy Beatley, and Heather Boyer, *Resilient Cities: Responding to Peak Oil and Climate Change* (Washington, D.C.: Island Press, 2009); Peter Newman and Isabella Jennings, *Cities as Sustainable Ecosystems: Principles and Practices* (Washington, D.C.: Island Press, 2008).

6 Robert Cervero, *The Transit Metropolis: A Global Inquiry* (Washington, D.C.: Island Press, 1998); Jeff Speck, *The Walkable City: How Downtown Can Save America, One Step at a Time* (New York: North Point Press, 2012).

7 These reflect the fundamental move away from rational planning since the 1960s. A participatory planning model that involves citizens in planning and design decision-making processes and promotes a sense of community has taken the place of one which privileged technical expertise. Sherry R. Arnstein, "A Ladder of Citizen Participation," *Journal of the American Institute of Planners* 35, no. 4 (1969): 216–24; Paul Davidoff, "Advocacy and Pluralism in Planning," *Journal of the American Institute of Planners* 31, no. 4 (1965): 331–38.

8 Richard Jackson and Stacy Sinclair, *Designing Healthy Communities* (San Francisco: John Wiley & Sons, 2012); Andrew Dannenberg, Howard Frumkin, and Richard Jackson, eds., *Making Healthy Places: Designing and Building for Health, Well-being, and Sustainability* (Washington, D.C.: Island Press, 2011); Ann Forsyth, Emily Salomon, and Laura Smead, *Creating Healthy Neighborhoods: Evidence-based Planning and Design Strategies* (Chicago: APA Planners Press / Routledge, 2017).

9 Ray Olderburg, *The Great Good Place: Cafes, Coffee Shops, Bookstores, Bars, Hair Salons, and Other Hangouts at the Heart of a Community* (New York: Marlowe & Company, 1989); Jan Gehl, *Life Between Buildings: Using Public Space* (Washington, D.C.: Island Press, 1987); Jan Gehl, *Cities for People* (Washington, D.C.: Island Press, 2010).

10 Since the early 1990s, several planning and design strategies have emerged, such as Smart Growth, New Urbanism, Landscape Urbanism, Sustainable Urbanism, and Tactical Urbanism, to name a few. Much has also been written on urban design principles and techniques for placemaking. Framework Thinking is intended to complement these rich conversations without being a manual. Key references include Jay Walliasper, *The Great Neighborhood Book: A Do-It-Yourself Guide to Placemaking* (Gabriola Island, B.C.: New Society Publishers, 2007); Andres Duany, Jeff Speck, and Mike Lydon, *The Smart Growth Manual* (New York: McGraw Hill, 2009); Peter Katz, *The New Urbanism: Towards an Architecture of Community* (New York: McGraw Hill, 1993); Charles Waldheim, *Landscape as Urbanism: A General Theory* (New Jersey: Princeton University Press, 2016); Laurie Olin et al, *Olin: Placemaking* (New York: Monacelli Press, 2008); Urban Design London, *The Design Companion for Planning and Placemaking* (London: RIBA Publishing, 2017); Jeff Speck, *Walkable City Rules: 101 Steps to Making Better Places* (Washington, D.C.: Island Press 2018); Derek Thomas, *Placemaking: An Urban Design Methodology* (New York: Routledge, 2016); Galina Tachieva, *Sprawl Repair Manual* (Washington, D.C.: Island Press, 2010).

11 Wendell Berry, *The Unsettling of America: Culture & Agriculture* (Berkeley, CA: Counterpoint, 2015 reprint of 1977 Original).

12 Mark Roseland, *Towards Sustainable Communities: Solutions for Citizens and Their Government* (Canada: New Society for Publishers, 2012); Kent Portney, *Taking Sustainable Cities Seriously: Economic Development, the Environment, and Quality of Life in American Cities* (Cambridge, MA: MIT Press, 2013); David R. Godschalk, "Land Use Planning Challenges: Coping with Conflicts in Visions of Sustainable Development and Livable Communities," *Journal of the American Planning Association* 70, no. 1 (2004): 5–13.

13 National Oceanic and Atmospheric Administration, "Living Shorelines," retrieved from https://www.habitatblueprint.noaa.gov/ living-shorelines/; Jeff

Goodell, *The Water Will Come: Rising Seas, Sinking Cities, and the Remaking of the Civilized World* (New York: Back Bay Books, 2017); Paula Mang and Ben Haggard, *Regenesis, Regenerative Development and Design: A Framework for Evolving Sustainability* (New York: Wiley & Sons, 2016).

14 Shlomo Angel et al, Atlas of Urban Expansion – 2016 Edition. Volume 1: Areas and Densities & Volume 2: Blocks and Roads Urban Expansion Program at New York University, UN-Habitat, and the Lincoln Institute of Land Policy, 2016), https://www.lincoln-inst.edu/sites/default/files/pubfiles/atlas-of-urban-expansion

15 "Placemaking: What If We Built Our Cities Around Places?," Project for Public Spaces, accessed February 19, 2024, https://uploads-ssl.webflow.com/5810e16fbe876c-ec6bcbd86e/6335ddc88fbf7f-29ec537d49_2022%20placemaking%20booklet.pdf

16 Peter G. Northouse, *Leadership: Theory and Practice* (Thousand Oaks, CA: Sage Publications, 2018).

17 Martine Haas and Mark Mortensen, 2016, "The Secrets of Great Teamwork," *Harvard Business Review* 94, no. 6 (2016): 70–117.

18 Rosabeth M. Kanter, "Zoom In, Zoom Out: The Best Leaders Know When To Focus In and When To Pull Back," *Harvard Business Review* 89, no. 3 (2011): 112–16.

19 Doris Kearns Goodwin, *Leadership in Turbulent Times* (New York: Simon & Schuster, 2018), 234–35.

20 "About Prairie Crossing," Prairie Crossing, accessed February 7, 2024, https://prairiecrossing.com/about/

21 Jane Gillette, "Mystical Mountains," *Landscape Architecture Magazine*, March 1996 86(3): 66–73.

22 Gillette, "Mystical Mountains," 66–73.

23 "Our Story: A Mountain Built by Community," Crystal Mountain Resort, accessed October 22, 2024, https://www.crystalmountain.com/your-visit/our-story/

24 Architects from Bull Stockwell Allen joined the team in the most recent 2023-2024 design workshop and master plan update. "Development Timeline," Crystal Mountain Resort, accessed October 22, 2024, https://www.crystalmountain realty.com/development-timeline/

25 "What is Placemaking?" Project for Public Spaces, accessed January 20, 2023, https://www.pps.org/article/what-is-placemaking; "Creative Placemaking, Placekeeping, and Cultural Strategies to Resist Displacement," U.S. Department of Arts and Culture, accessed January 20, 2023, https://usdac.us/blogac/2017/12/11/creative-placemaking-placekeeping-and-cultural-strategies-to-resist-displacement .

26 "Holland's Heated Sidewalk Streets Were a Gamble That Seems to Have Paid Off," Michigan Public/NPR, accessed November 6, 2023, https://www.michiganradio.org/families-community/2016-03-22/hollands-heated-sidewalks-streets-were-a-gamble-that-seems-to-have-paid-off

27 "Snowmelt: A Snow-Free Holland," Holland Area Convention & Visitors Bureau, accessed November 6, 2023, https://www.holland.org/snow-free-holland#:~:text=Snowmelt%20was%20first%20implemented%20in,underneath%20the%20streets%20and%20 sidewalks

28 Greg Holcombe, email message to authors, November 2, 2023.

29 Dwight Eisenhower, "Remarks at the National Defense Executive Reserve Conference," November 14, 1957, accessed November 2, 2023, https://www.presidency.ucsb.edu/documents/remarks-the-national-defense-executive-reserve-conference

30 Daryl Van Tongeren, *Humble: Free Yourself from the Traps of a Narcissistic World* (New York: The Experiment, 2022), 11-13.

31 Norman Wirzba, *The Agrarian Spirit: Cultivating Faith, Community, and the Land* (South Bend, IN: University of Notre Dame Press, 2022), 138.

32 Brené Brown, *Atlas of the Heart: Mapping Meaningful Connection and the Language of the Human Experience* (New York: Random House, 2021), xxi.

33 "Racial Equity Plan of Action," American Society of Landscape Architects, accessed January 23, 2023, https://www.asla.org/racialequity-plan.aspx ; "Guides for Equitable Practice," American Institute of Architects, accessed January 23, 2023, https://content.aia.org/sites/default/files/2021-06/AIA_Guides_for_Equitable_Practice_08_Engaging_Community.pdf ; "Equity, Diversity, Inclusion," American Planning Association, accessed January 23, 2023, https://www.planning.org/equity/ .

34 Epictetus, *Enchiridion, in The Art of Living: The Classic Manual on Virtue, Happiness, and Effectiveness*, trans. Sharon Lebell (New York: HarperCollins, 1995), 10.

William ("Bill") J. Johnson, FASLA

WILLIAM J. JOHNSON, FASLA, is one of the cofounders of Johnson, Johnson & Roy, Inc. (JJR)—a multi-office international design practice before it merged with SmithGroup. He is a professor emeritus of the University of Michigan where he served as professor of landscape architecture, and the dean of the School of Natural Resources from 1975 to 1983.

Through the years, Bill has focused on issues of environmental design working in multiple roles: as planner, designer, teacher, and academic administrator. A landscape architect by training, his early interests focused on broad-scale land development/protection strategies. He pioneered cross-disciplinary ways of working in fitting land development programs to sensitive environmental conditions. His practice has ranged across projects of regional and community planning, urban design, long-range campus development, natural resource, and historic preservation. His contributions emphasize the balancing of social, cultural, and environmental values in expansive problem-solving initiatives.

After Bill's tenure at the University of Michigan, he formed a Berkeley partnership with Harvard classmate Peter Walker (1992–1997). As the Peter Walker William Johnson and Partners (PWWJ) office, they consulted on assignments throughout the country and in Japan. In Seattle, Bill devoted much of his consulting time as mentor and critic for the architectural firm of NBBJ.

A trailblazing giant who shaped multiple generations of practitioners and educators, Bill received several awards in his career: the American Society for Landscape Architecture's Gold Medal (1986), the Lifetime Achievement Award from the Council of Educators in Landscape Architecture (2019), the Landscape Architecture Foundation Medal (2020), and the Harvard Graduate School of Design Distinguished Alumni Award (2023).

Har Ye Kan, AICP

DR. HAR YE KAN, AICP, is a community planner, teacher, and sojourner. She grew up in the garden city of Singapore and is a blend of her Asian roots and global perspectives. After moving from the New England area to Holland, Michigan, she crossed paths with Bill Johnson, who inspired her to shift fully into community planning and design.

Through her West Michigan-based practice, Har Ye collaborates in multidisciplinary teams across various project types and scales. At the heart of her approach is a mission to create places reflecting their unique contexts, stories, and potential, while fostering harmony between people and place. Her work includes housing, neighborhood and community design, suburban retrofits, long-range campus planning, historic preservation of cultural landscapes, and parks/nature preserve planning.

Outside her practice, Har Ye has taught at Harvard University, Dartmouth College, and Hope College. Together with Peter Rowe and Ann Forsyth, she co-authored two books—*Urban Intensities: Contemporary Housing Types and Territories* (2014) and *China's Urban Communities: Concepts, Contexts, and Wellbeing* (2016).

Har Ye received her doctorate from the Harvard University Graduate School of Design, a master's in Regional Studies-East Asia from the Harvard University Graduate School of Arts & Sciences, and her bachelor's degree in Geography from the University of Cambridge.